G000056750

THE VIBRANT FAMILY

Other titles in the
Systemic Thinking and Practice Series:
edited by Ros Draper
published and distributed by Karnac

Credit card orders, Tel: +44(0) 20-7431-1075; Fax: +44(0) 20 7435 9076
Email: shop@karnacbooks.com
www.karnacbooks.com

Kirsten Seidenfaden
Piet Draiby
Susanne Søborg Christensen
Vibeke Hejgaard
Edited by Mette-Marie Davidsen and Ros Draper

THE
VIBRANT
FAMILY

A HANDBOOK FOR PARENTS AND PROFESSIONALS

KARNAC

First English edition published in 2011 by
Karnac Ltd
118 Finchley Road, London NW3 5HT

Copyright © 2011 to Kirsten Seidenfaden and Piet Draiby

First published in 2007 by TV2

Published in Danish as *Det levende familie* by
Lindhardt og Ringhof Forlag A/S © 2009

All rights reserved. No part of this publication may be reproduced,
stored in a retrieval system, or transmitted, in any form or by any means,
electronic, mechanical, photocopying, recording, or otherwise,
without the prior written permission of the publisher.

British Library Cataloguing in Publication Data
A C.I.P. for this book is available from the British Library
    ISBN: 978-1-85575-818-6

The book was written in close co-operation with journalist and writer
Mette-Marie Davidsen.
The English version is edited in close co-operation with Ros Draper.

All illustrations in the book are by the artist Viktor IV.
They have been reproduced in agreement with Ina Elisabeth Munck.

Portrait of the authors: Miklos Szabo
Cover and graphics: Bramsen and Nørgaard
Translation by James Bulman-May

Edited and produced by The Studio Publishing Services Ltd
www.publishingservicesuk.co.uk
email: studio@publishingservicesuk.co.uk

Printed in Great Britain

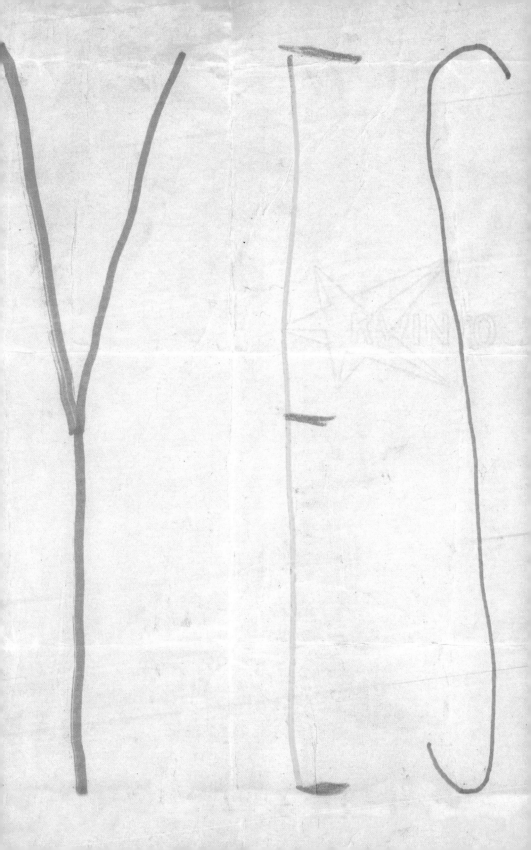

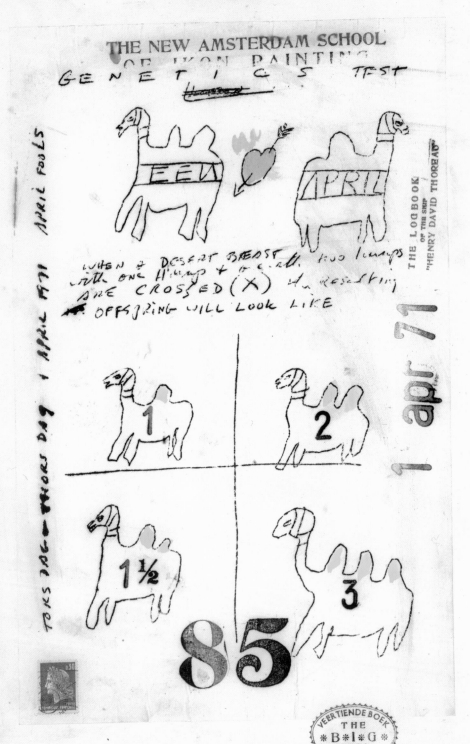

TABLE OF CONTENTS

Now

BEHANDELD 3 1 JAN. 1970

DEAR FERDINAND III   I JUST POSTED YOU A LETTER THIS MORNING AND
I HAVE MADE SOME PAPERS FOR THE BOOK WITH YOU AS SUBJECT   AND I
THINK IF YOU LIKE THEIDEA I WROTE THIS MORNING MUCH BETTER TO FINESH
WHAT IS TO BE DONE IN NEW YORK AND COME OVER TO YOUR SHIP AS SOON AS
POSSIBLE AND ENJOY A FEW DAYS ON THE SHIP IN   WINTER   AND I THINK IT
WILL BE TOO COLD FOR YOU OF COURSE BUT AT LEAST YOU KNOW IT AND WE
TAKE THE TRUCK FOR A H O L I D A Y   ANDLIVE AN ADVENTURE FATHER AND
SON AND I RECORD IT FOR THE BOOK AND I AM CERTAIN WE WILL HAVE A
VERY ALIVE EXPERIENCE ANDIT WILL COST ALMOST NOTHING   YOU ARE
MUCH TGALR ...... AN YOU GIVE YOURSELF ~~KREEDT~~ CREDIT   I KNOW BECAUSE I
TAKE .... UP YOUR OWN POSSIBILITIES

..... IS ANOTHER MORE STRIKING MATTER   YOU WRITE HOW JIMMY IS DOING H
ITS BEST .... EXACTLY .... THAT LINE MEANS   AND YOUREMEMBER HER
..... KILLING YOU ... OWN FATHER ... THE APARTMENT HERE ONCE SHE WORE
..... ANDCOM ... INK OF THE LIFE THAT ~~IXX~~ HAS CAUSED HER TO TURN INTO
A ..... OF SUBHUMAN NOT POTENTIAL MONSTER   WILMA IS NOT DOING THIS TO
H ...... LIFE HAS DONE THIS .... ER   YOU NEVER HAD ANY HIGH
EXPECT .... YOUR LACK OF FORMAL EDUCATION
TO BE YOUR CUSHION .... INARY ... PAINTINGS AND THIS PROTECTED YOU
BUT WILMA HAD VERY ... AND WAS NOT SO CLEVER TO SEE
WHAT WAS ... THE FAN ... AND SO WHAT ... BROKEN HER
AND NOW ... A PATCHED UP READY TO EX ... ITY
AND WHERE ... THE RESPONSIBILITY? HAVE YOU PRO ... ORMALITY
OF A CHILD AND ... WOMAN IN WILMA NO ... IS THE ... SHE MADE
THAT DEST ... HE ... THE MENTAL HOSPITALS ... SUI ... ND WHAT CANNOT
WALK SAF ... ON ... STREET FOR EVERYONE TH .... IS
THERE ARE ... IN THEIR HOMES JUST ... IS NOT
STRICTLY NECESSARY TH ... BROUGHT TO THE .... WILMA IS ... LD
ONE OF THOSE HOME HOSPITAL ... WHEN YOU LOOK AT HER ... OLD
AND CHILDREN THEN YOU WONDER ... THIS COULD HAPPEN IT LOOKS ... ODD
DOES IT NOT THEN TAKE A GOOD LOOK AT WILMA   AND THEN WONDER W ...
HER TROUBLE CAME FROM WAS SHE BORN WITH IT? ... NO THERE IS NOTHING
WRONG WITH TH ... BLOOD YOU AND MY MOTHER G ... TO US WILMA ENTERED TH
AMERICAN LIFE AN AMERICAN (YOU NOT IMMIGRANT SOMEHOW MEANS SECOND
CLASS AND YOU ACCEPTED THAT   HERE I AM IMMIGRANT ANDI DO NOT ACCEPT
SECOND CLASS BUT THIS IS NOT AMERICA BUT THAT IS ANOTHER STORY

BACK TO WILMA ... AING THE AMERICAN LIFE AND I TRAVELED IT AND STOOD
BESIDE IT FOR ... LONG TIME AND FINALLY LEFT IT IN ORDER TO ... MY
OWN LIFE   AND NOT THE GROUPTHINK FORM OF LIFE THAT LIFE ... TI
VE ... FERDINAN ... M ... NY VICTIMS

AND ... NEW YORK YOU ... LL TER IS NOTHING TO A ... ON JIMMY ...
H ... CH ... ND LIV ... H ... CHILD IN H ... O V ... OUGH IT MY NO ...
LONG ... H M N UNPL ... SANT M MOR ... "JIMMY IS DOING
HIS BEST" ETC ... BUT HE IS PART OF THE CHOICE AND IS A FOOL AND DOES
NOT KNOW THE DANGERS FOR IT IS ALL SUCH A PRETTY SEEMING PACKAGE
BUT YOU MUST THINK ABOUT IT SERIOUSLY FOR YOU KNOW THE UP RINGING
AND THERE IIS NOTHING WRONG WITH THE "BLOOD" BASICALLY WHAT ARE KNOWN
AS MENTAL PATIENTS ARE FOR THE MOST PART SIMPLY WH ... PERSOJS WHO HAVE
BEEN VICTIMIZED BY THE STRONG   WILMA IS THE VICTIM ... JAQUELINE
KENNEDY AMONGST MANY OTHERS AND THAT IS WHY SHE SPOKE HER NAMR SO
OFTEN   THAT MRS KENNEDY OR ONASSIS DOES NOT KNOW WILMA DOESNT ... N
TO KNOW HER IS EXACTLY TO THE POINT
BUT WALTER LEFT THAT SYSTEM AND SO HE HARDLY KNOWS MRS O EXISTS
AND IN A WAY SHE DOES NOT EXIST FOR HIM AND SO HE DOES NOT SCREAM
ABOUT MRS O BUT MAKES POEMS TO HE SUN AND COLORS THEM IN

WRITE ME SOON   WE TAKE A TRIP SOON TOGETHER   YES?

P S i just come back from the waterloo market i found many old books
laying on ground i ripped off the covers and will make drawn ikons
on the inside where there is white paperxxx always very simple
work i am jumping around and over the ship as if i were still 14
years ols and you know i still am   you are as young as you can
allow with safety and you are not o l d

THE LOGBOOK
OF THE SHIP
"HENRY DAVID THOREAU"

EERSTE BOEK
THE
CANCEL
SUN

SERIES EDITOR'S FOREWORD

*T*he *Vibrant Family* was first published in Denmark in 2009, where it was well received by lay people, the media, and professionals alike. The themes in the book are, however, universal for families wherever they are, particularly first-world families, and not just Danish families. This book is, therefore, a timely and welcome addition to the series.

It is particularly timely as it has been fashionable in the past few years to speak of the need to integrate ideas in the world of psychotherapy across theories and modalities.

This book offers a synthesis of ideas from current research in developmental psychology, neuroscience, and psychotherapy, as well as showing how contemporary ideas, such as mentalization, can be linked to attachment and narrative ideas which remain contemporary, but first appeared in twentieth-century psycho-therapy literature.

The book is particularly welcome because the authors, two of Denmark's most experienced and well-known psychotherapists, have succeeded in writing a book for parents as well as pro-fessionals. Complex ideas are elegantly expressed in everyday language without losing the depth of the insights being offered to readers.

It is no mean feat to communicate complex ideas in an easily accessible and convincing way. The authors' ability to connect many ideas together to create, as it were, a 'meta map' show us the extent of their combined experience, wisdom, and passion for their work. This passion is echoed both in the *Vibrant* in the title and the aesthetic appeal of the book, beautifully illustrated by the internationally recognized artist Viktor IV. As one Danish reviewer said: 'Only rarely does a book fall into your hands that is so inviting and so beautifully illustrated that you feel like giving it to your friends for aesthetic reasons'. *The Vibrant Family* and its companion volume, *The Vibrant Relationship, A Handbook for Couples and Therapists*, published earlier in 2011 in this series, are such books.

The core concept in the book is the crucial role of acknowledgement or recognition in creating and sustaining, nurturing family relationships. The importance of acknowledgement and recognition for empathic and nurturing relationships is relatively easy to understand, but more difficult to put into practice. The authors introduce readers to the useful tool of 'The Acknowledging Dialogue' as a way of enacting, and learning when necessary, the attunement central to attachment and narrative ideas and the capacity for mentalization.

The use throughout the book of transcripts from family interactions demonstrating the use of the acknowledging dialogue bring these ideas alive and, I hope, will whet readers' appetites to add this tool to their repertoire of skills, whether they are parents, children, grandparents, or professionals.

The sequence of the chapters in the book takes into account both the generational aspects of family life and the life-cycle stages of the family, from an early chapter entitled 'When Lovers Become Parents' to the final chapter, entitled 'Acknowledging Relationships with Grandparents'. Well-documented developmental themes such as attachment and exploration are discussed, with supporting evidence from recent research in neuroscience, in the chapters entitled 'Attachment and Exploration in Focus' and 'The Brain—Our Invisible Greenhouse'.

The authors say this is not a book about how to raise healthy and confident children, but a book explaining how recognizing the family behaviour patterns that connect and disconnect through the lens of the acknowledging dialogue can resolve conflict in relationships and promote intimacy in family relationships. Systemic practitioners train long and hard to develop skills in tracking distance and closeness in family interactions and in enabling family members to share with one another their stories about intimacy or lack of intimacy in their life together.

Often a good outcome in therapy is when family members become able to talk honestly to one another about how connected or disconnected they feel to one another and what it is they yearn for in their relationships with one another. The acknowledging dialogue and intimacy explained and described in this book will I hope be a useful addition to the skills parents, grandparents and children claim as essential when they tell their stories of relationships enjoyed, repaired or endured. For psychotherapists working with families, couples and individuals familiarity with the ideas and skills in this book will hopefully enhance their ability to create safe spaces in which clients can talk with one another and professionals about talking and about relationships.

Ros Draper
Hampshire, 2011

A s parents, we have probably all experienced a burning desire to pass on the best of what we have in order to promote our child's healthy development. We want to see him or her grow up as a sensitive and emotionally well-balanced person, and also as a resourceful and robust human being with a well-developed capacity to cope with life's many challenges, a person whose life with his or her loved ones is full of happy moments as infinite as the stars.

We are also all familiar with situations, events, or stages in our lives where we do not quite feel that we have succeeded as parents or partners.

This is the reason why we wrote *The Vibrant Family* for all parents who are ready to develop those aspects of themselves that their children need in order to have the best possible start in life. In our view, parenthood is a unique opportunity not just to create a family, but also to create growth and development in our own lives, as well as in the lives of our children and with others with whom we are intimate.

The Vibrant Family is a manual based on the new paradigms that have inspired us in our professional and personal lives. We have an optimistic approach, and would like to invite you and your partner to develop some of the aspects of your selves that we believe are crucial to your child's development. Reading this book, you will also be in the process of developing your own relationship in quite a unique way. One of the central points of the book is that when we work well together as partners in parenting, we also become capable of supporting and helping each other when the stress level, the frustration, and the despair escalate, and the ability and the desire for intimacy have vanished. One of the messages of this book is that we, as parents, must take responsibility for all the emotions in the family environment – including those that exist between us as a couple. All too often, we forget that our children live and are shaped in the atmosphere we, the adults, create in the family!

The purpose of this book, *The Vibrant Family* (like its companion volume *The Vibrant Relationship*), is to focus on the importance and centrality of developing an "acknowledging intimacy" through dialogue. Briefly, the sole aim of this book is to demonstrate that an "acknowledging intimacy" initiates growth and also enhances development of the brain. "Acknowledging intimacy" is another way of describing the intangible concept of love: the blissful state we desire to find with our partner and which we all yearn to live in and pass on to our children. If we do not have it, we long for it: the "acknowledging intimacy".

In this book, we attempt to show you that what we call the miracle of acknowledgement is quite easy to understand. But, like all other ideas requiring us to change, it can be difficult to initiate. Based on our own therapeutic and personal experiences, we want to pass on quite simple ways to apply the new knowledge about "acknowledging intimacy". We describe ways in which we can act in more confident, meaningful ways that enhance development with the people who are closest to us. Only when we move out of the "me bubble" and into the "we community" does it actually become possible to help each other to move on when life is challenging and stressful.

Acknowledgement means a willingness to see the world through the eyes of the other for a while, thereby giving the other the experience of being deeply understood. A specific kind of social skill, which is this ability to share other people's state of mind, is central to the "acknowledging intimacy". It is a state of mind which we aspire to practise continually as a way of life.

The Vibrant Family is inspired by a wide range of personal and professional experiences, supported by research which seems to confirm the same profound principle: that a calm, acknowledging intimacy is the basis of all psychological development and also enhances brain development and function – two sides of the same coin – from birth to the mature, well-functioning human being. Using this perspective, we humbly stand on the shoulders of all the others who have been, and are, interested in having "the mind in mind" in their relationships.

This book is addressed to parents who live with their biological children as well as to parents with children of different marriages, divorced parents, grandparents, and all other adults who have close family ties. In our experience, the attitudes, points of view, and suggested actions that are described in this book may also be valuable for all other committed relationships.

Finally, it is important to us to point out that the thoughts about, and the attitudes to, development that we express can also be found in various kinds of counselling and therapy. The couples, the parents, or the families who find inspiration in this book and wish to gather further up-to-date information, or who might have difficulties that need to be addressed, can find more information at:
www.thevibrantfamily.dk

The authors would like to thank Mette-Marie Davidsen for a wonderful, unfailing, persevering, and always inspiring co-operation. Also thanks to Ina Elisabeth Munck for her enthusiasm and for once again generously making Victor's subtle *oeuvre* available as a sounding board to our text. We also wish to thank our clients for their hopes and steps to make their own as well as their children's dreams come true. Thank you.

Kirsten Seidenfaden, Piet Draiby,
Susanne Søborg Christensen, and Vibeke Hejgaard

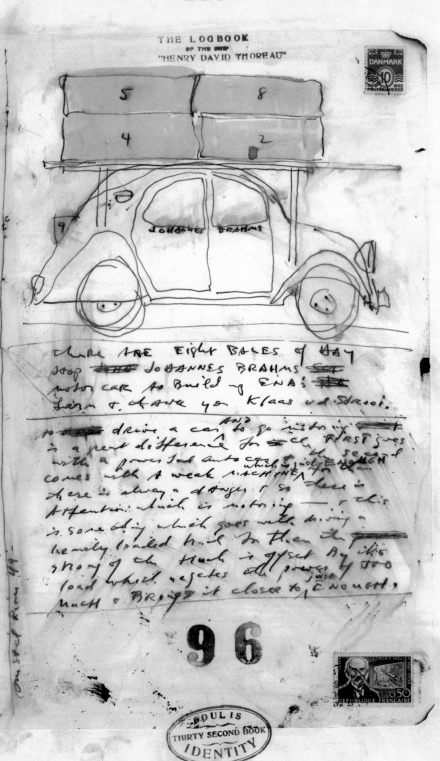

THERE ARE EIGHT BALES OF HAY
STOP ~~THE~~ JOHANNES BRAHMS ~~SET~~
MOTOR CAR TO BUILD A ENAS ~~THE~~
LARON + LEAVE YOU KLAAS VD SCHROON

~~TO DRIVE~~ drive a car AND to go motoring
is a great difference for the FIRST goes
with a powered auto car which is just ENOUGH
comes with a weak MACHINE for the
there is always a danger so there is
Attention which is motoring — + this
is something which goes with driving a
heavily loaded truck for then the
strong of the truck is offset by the
load which rejects the power by too
much + BRINGS it closer to, ENOUGH.

96

THE VIBRANT FAMILY

M ost children live with their biological parents. This fact covers, to our knowledge the developed countries but is most certainly culturally dependent. This is probably surprising, since there is a tendency to focus on the divorces, the single parents, and the children living in blended families as opposed to the nuclear family. The biological family is, thereby, still the framework in which most children grow up. However, this statistic does not reveal how parents and children thrive individually and with each other.

Much research into human growth and development confirms that in this day and age more children than ever before are thriving. This is wonderful news, but in no way should it detract from the focus on the group of children and young people who have suffered and do not thrive. Fortunately, this group is much more visible these days than previously. We now speak openly about the fact that various types of parental abuse and neglect contribute to children's and young adults' failure to thrive. These are the children that encounter difficulties later in life.

It is important to emphasize the fact that even though the conditions of children in general have improved, this does not mean that all are having the wonderful time that most parents wish for their children. Throughout the three or four decades of our professional careers working with couples and children, we have seen a great change in the ways in which children and young people develop. Over the years, we have experienced how children who, in previous years, typically would be quiet, withdrawn, and slightly anxious, have, to a greater extent, become responsive and highly visible. One reason could be that all the children who used to suffer from anxiety have now become parents. With the best of intentions, they now attempt to spare their children experiences that they found harmful and problematic when they were children. The result could, for instance, be very well-intentioned parents who might be unclear in the matter of setting boundaries, or parents with very fixed opinions and a great tendency to want to control. One common thread that links all parental behaviour is that it is informed by their own childhood experiences and not based solely on their recognition of their child's needs. The view tends to be: *my child should certainly never attend a bad school, or my child should never experience the insecurity I felt as a child.*

In our view, it is now possible to extract the "essential vitamins" from our cumulative body of knowledge and introduce them into the daily diet of families. It is our profound wish that *The Vibrant Family* will introduce you to new, evidence-based knowledge of what we call the acknowledging intimacy. This concept is vital, not just to our child's development, but also for us as parents and couples. Little by little, we are giving up the idea that we, as parents, must solve problems, give good advice, and constantly stimulate our children's growth. Instead, we are moving towards a realization of the fact that if only we listen in an acknowledging way and are prepared to change our behaviour to ensure that we are present in loving and unconditional ways, then we will create the best possible foundation for children, parenthood, family, and relationships.

ACKNOWLEDGING INTIMACY GENERATES LOVE

We are all aware of the great importance to adults and children of nourishing food, fresh air, plenty of exercise, and an unstressed way of life. In our time, some families with young children have become very good at navigating the waters of family life in accordance with these parameters. However, getting the external environment right should not be undertaken at the cost of the emotional environment that each of us has within us and between us; it is the emotional environment that influences our way of life more than anything else.

This book provides answers to questions we may have as to how we can become more conscious of our emotional environment, our roles as parents, and how we inadvertently influence our children in ways that are controlled by our own unresolved emotions. Finally, the book points to simple ways we, as adults, can create an emotional environment and ways of being together that will help our children to develop self-esteem and self-acceptance, so that they, in turn, can experience the fullest possible development of their talents and personality.

Many parents do not realize that we do not produce better families by allowing interaction to take place on the children's terms alone, or by glossing over the problems and the vulnerable areas in our relationships. We ignore the importance of functioning well with our partner and letting our combined efforts create a solid foundation of confidence, empathy, respect, and tenderness which will allow us to live a stress-free, calm, and intimate life with our children.

We have selected acknowledging intimacy – the jewel in the crown of the mind – as a term for the process that can create miracles between two adults who love each other and between parents and their children. Recent research confirms that acknowledging intimacy is the most important gift we can give our children. A wide range of experience and research confirms that calm acknowledging intimacy is the basis of all development of the emotions and the brain in the infant as well as in the adult. We would like to communicate this knowledge in a way that can be understood by everyone, and that can be applied by us as parents and with our partners in our daily lives. The point is that the way in which we are with each other as parents is significant to our own individual development, as well as that of our partner

---

PRAISE DOES NOT EQUAL ACKNOWLEDGEMENT

Today there is a lot of emphasis on the importance of appreciation, praise, and acknowledgement. We would like to emphasize that there is a difference between these concepts. We can show appreciation of our partner and our children by praising them for certain things they do. Children as well as adults need encouragement in terms of appreciation/ praise and acknowledgement. The point here is that it is a both – and rather than an either-or – and we should be conscious of whether we are praising or acknowledging. The disadvantage of praise is that we can become dependent on it. On the other hand, when we experience acknowledgement, we are able to accept that other people are different from us. This helps us to know and understand ourselves and each other better. Instead, we believe parents should develop a universe of acknowledgement, in which the rights to be and express ourselves as the people we are, to think and feel as we do, are acknowledged.

---

and our children. This is the development – the we community – we undergo by virtue of living with others, learning how to handle conflicts and live together in spite of our differences. In this way, we give ourselves the best chance for a balanced, curious, and vibrant existence in the world. These are big words. As a minimum, we need the will to change our attitudes and ways of parenting. Then we need to work on these issues in our daily lives.

One of the clear messages, we hope, of this book is that it is the parents and not the children who need to change for the family to function. This is not a pedagogical project where we, as adults, have to learn how to address our children and how to behave towards them. If we really want to change and develop *joie de vivre* and dynamism in the family, we need to see ourselves as more than just parents. We are also, one hopes, partners in a love relationship in which our children conceived. It follows that the quality in the joint parenting can never be greater than that found in the relationship, the marriage, or the former marriage.

The parents' well-being is crucial to the development of the entire family. If the parents pollute the space and the air with their bickering, mutual criticism, silence, absence, or anger, their children need to find ways to learn how to behave in this compromised and loveless atmosphere. In order to be able to survive, children are forced to learn strategies with the sole purpose of helping them find ways to exist in the crossfire of parental quarrels, silence, or distance, or in the slipstream of the parents' lack of attention, acknowledgement, and understanding.

This might lead us to believe that we should be afraid of the conflicts in our relationship and try to avoid them. This is not the case. Conflicts and disagreements will always exist in all relationships and in all families. We should not worry about intense feelings such as anger, either. We should, however, be afraid of scenarios where we do not succeed in repairing the damage after our conflicts, as couples as well as parents. Nothing is more important than to restore intimacy and connection after major emotional meltdowns, silence, or embarrassing failures. Put in another way, we should patch things up and sweep the pieces up after us.

ACKNOWLEDGING INTIMACY

In terms of *acknowledging intimacy*, we would go as far as to assert that living together in such a way could be the goal of all human beings. *Acknowledging intimacy* may be the closest we get to the intangible concept of love: it is a blend of the ability to listen, empathize, reflect, understand, and, thus, liberate ourselves from old, damaging survival strategies, such as losing our temper, walking away, or staying in a bad mood.

The psychological term for what we call the *acknowledging intimacy* is mentalization, which has recently been the focus of much multi-disciplinary research. The term mentalization means the ability to feel and express our own emotions, thoughts, and bodily sensations, as well as being receptive to those same qualities in others. The crucial basis of *acknowledging intimacy* – the ability to mentalize – is primarily developed during the first three years of life, and it continues during the following 12–16 years.

First of all, the ability to create and remain in a state of *acknowledging intimacy* is closely associated with how good our parents and we as parents are at practising this way of being. Children are influenced by their environment and are dependent on their adults, who can best support them in the development of their ability to handle strain and maintain inner calm and balance through *acknowledging intimacy*.

Second, the good news from the world of research is that at any point we can develop and refine our ability to practise *acknowledging intimacy* for the rest of our lives. That means that we can continue to develop our own abilities to practise acknowledging intimacy, as well as that of our children, as second nature, so that it eventually becomes a lifestyle we follow unconsciously. It is necessary to work at our *acknowledging intimacy* continually, since it is not a resource that is accessible at all times. It decreases or disappears completely when we feel inadequate and powerless.

VIK
AMERICAN
IKONS
AMSTERDAM

A: YES

△ THE LOGBOOK
OF THE SHIP
"HENRY DAVID THOREAU"

BEHANDELD 0 5 MAART 1970

open (out, IN, & Middle)
structure

4 III 9 10 7

8 4 3   2   1   AF 2 3 R 4
                  1

Suggestion
the In, out, & Middle diagram

change:
the Out, IN,
the Out end to be left open & marked
    INFINITY. (∞)
YES / N is better — the form represents
    a total fixed now
the open structure is the layer?
    Layer train.
    THANK you
    Pauline

BEFORE

MADE IN HOLLAND

72

DERDE BOEK
Y·E·S

Our choice of the title, *The Vibrant Family*, is based on the premise of creating a more conscious way of maintaining a more vibrant couple relationship instead of contaminating our children with our old, unresolved childhood emotions. That means that this book does not deal with how to raise children, how to set limits, or a particular way in which to communicate with children. Instead, we focus on the reasons why well-being and security in the couple relationship are crucial if we want to raise confident, well-balanced children, and we describe ways of being in a relationship.

Using a special tool, which we call the *Acknowledging Dialogue*, and explaining the thinking behind this dialogue, first the parents and then the children, each from their own perspective, will be able to work steadily towards the goal of living together in *acknowledging intimacy*. The Acknowledging Dialogue generates an understanding and teaches adults to create an atmosphere and a way of communicating that can resolve conflicts in the relationships. When this happens, it automatically rubs off on the children's well-being and confidence, providing them with the necessary calm and trust to stay present with their full range of emotions, abilities, and personality.

The *Acknowledging Dialogue* is a particular form of structured dialogue with many different applications. When the Acknowledging Dialogue is developed, it can, in many situations, pave the way for a completely new way of being with all types of people. Essentially, the *Acknowledging Dialogue* is a tool that:

- teaches us to listen – to really listen – and place ourselves in the other person's shoes. This ability nourishes and encourages depth and understanding in any relationship

- helps us to access the psychological baggage we all carry from our childhood concerning the ways in which we live alongside other people. For better or for worse, these experiences unconsciously influence our parenting.

Willpower alone is not enough when we decide what kind of parent we want to be. We can only become different and better parents by practising new ways of behaving, with the intention of creating a vibrant, insightful relationship, or, if we are single parents, a vibrant and perceptive relationship to our self and our surroundings.

- teaches us a new way of recognizing our feelings so that we can learn to be angry, afraid, or sad in ways that do not make our children or partners feel insecure or anxious. Not only do we learn how to take responsibility for our emotions, but we also learn to take responsibility for the emotions in the shared space of our relationships.

- teaches us to move out of the "me" bubble and into a "we" community, where it is possible to help each other move on in times of trouble.

When we use the acknowledging way of thinking and dialogue, as couples and as parents we have a unique opportunity to develop our role as parents: while helping our child, we are also developing our relationship and ourselves.

ALMOST LIKE A MASSAGE

. . . We were closer to a point of no return than ever before in the twelve years we have been together. Gitte felt lonely and unhappy and became increasingly distant with the children. I missed a fully present partner and felt frustrated at being left on my own with child rearing. In the old days, we would get angry with each other and Gitte would cry her heart out when we disagreed about how to raise the children. Now, Gitte had begun to withdraw into herself and remain quiet when we disagreed about anything. The atmosphere in the entire family was gloomy and influenced by the silence.

We realized that we had to make some drastic changes in order to mend the situation. The parallel lives, where we buried ourselves in work – *you make your clothes, then I will make my music* – was the beginning of the end. If we continued in this way, each with our own agendas and two different ideas of what it takes to make a real family, then we would not have a chance.

We also knew that if our future was to have a chance, we would have to address our problems together. We have focused intensely on doing this. Doing something important together was essentially what we both wanted. We chose to pool our resources and work our way towards establishing *acknowledging intimacy* in our lives. One of the ways we did this was to learn to use the *Acknowledging Dialogue*.

Before we began, we were at odds with each other in quite childish ways. *When you do not want to listen to me, then I do not want to listen to you.* Now that we have adopted the acknowledging approach as second nature, we are instead able to give each other some hints, such as *you know what I mean*. We refer to shared themes in perceptive ways and support each other. In this way, we have become much better at avoiding misunderstandings and avoiding having the same old dogfights.

This has had a direct effect on our children. To give an example, we have always had a great deal of unrest and trouble at mealtimes. Today, we see that this is, to a greater extent, determined by the way the adults interact rather than by what happens between the children. For instance, I become annoyed when Gitte comments on the way I eat, and the children feel insecure. I become very angry and stubborn when I am criticized. The children sense this and fill the room with hyped-up energy and tension. I would like to alter my eating habits; to eat less and at a slower pace. This is no doubt related to the way my father ate. We were three boys and we were all voracious eaters. The meal was just something that should be over and done with. I always wanted it to be different in my own family, but as long as I am criticized, I cannot do so.

These days we relate to each other differently. We allow each other more space to express our differences. The peaceful dialogue between the adults at the table has rubbed off on the children, who are now calmer. The fact that we are able to communicate in another way and solve the problems that used to escalate into conflicts has created a completely different and wonderful dynamic in our family.

We particularly notice how much an expectant and listening attitude means to Emil, our eldest, who is six years old. We have experienced problematic episodes, where Emil has had difficulties expressing himself and has rolled around on the floor, screaming. We still have episodes, but not to the same extent as before. When he was in that mood, he was sent away to be on his own for a while. This has changed, however. When we began to have a more listening attitude, it struck us that he began to tell us much more about his experiences. Among other things, he told us how shameful it was for him to sit on the bench – the doghouse – and how difficult it was for him to return from the bench and re-enter the community of other children. Hence, I talk a great deal with him about how he can avoid sitting on the bench. Yesterday, he told us for the first time in a long time that he had had a wonderful day. . . and that he had not been on the bench at all.

It is strange how little one actually has to do in order to change the atmosphere. It is fantastic. We are very aware that we have two extremely active kids, but the fact that we have found a new calm and a new strength has stabilized them in amazing ways. It has also provided us with an indescribable energy. Previously, we were unable to accomplish anything; now we have lots of energy. We talk a lot about how we can hold on to the *Acknowledging Dialogue*, because it is just like getting a massage. We have discovered that it takes constant attention to create the good quality intimacy we all need.

Jens

To some parents, this book may be a disturbing experience, since it may provoke new thoughts of what we could have done differently instead of what we did. This is certainly an issue that we had in mind when we wrote the book. Quite a few of us are, and have been, in the same situation. There should be room, of course, for such disturbing thoughts, and we recommend sharing these thoughts with your partner, as we have done in the writing process. Our profound hope is that the reader comes to the realization that it is never too late to be part of creating the foundation of a vibrant family.

In short, we think that parenthood based on *acknowledging intimacy* – no matter how old our children are – is a unique chance for all of us to give and receive love, to create intimacy and confidence, and a daily life in which we all thrive. Introducing the *acknowledging intimacy* into our lives does not just create a win–win situation, but actually a quadruple win–win-win–win situation. The reason is that *acknowledging intimacy* is pure gold for your child, yourself, your partner, and your relationship. So why not take that chance?

The Vibrant Family is divided into nine chapters. The first chapters introduce you to various frames of references used by professionals. These provide a comprehensive understanding of the reasons why it is second nature to some of us to live in *acknowledging intimacy*, while it is awfully difficult for others. The same ideas also provide us with an answer as to how we can learn to develop an *acknowledging intimacy*, even if we were not introduced to this way of communicating when we were children. The ideas also explain how we can pass this important gift on to our children. The frames of references are:

- The ways we form attachments to other people (Attachment Theory)
- The way our brain develops and functions (Neurobiology)
- The ways we talk about our emotions and experiences (Narrative Theory, acknowledging pedagogics and psychology, and the *Marte Meo* method).

The remaining chapters of the book describe how we can learn to apply the *Acknowledging Dialogue* in our daily lives with our partner and our children. Here, we share well-documented and practical tools, including the *Acknowledging Dialogue* for Parents, which all couples and parents can use. We will introduce the reader to tools and understandings which, in our own professional and personal lives, have turned out to be gateways to a rich, confident, and valuable life for quite a number of adults and children.

For those who would like to dig deeper into the ideas presented, the text also supplies professional background information and references. However, these are not crucial to the understanding and the application of the ideas in this book. The coloured boxes all contain statements and stories from real life, and are told by families who are using the acknowledging approach described in this book.

In addition, several chapters end with a list of questions for you, which we call "reflections". You are welcome to immerse yourself into them or dip into them later when you feel like it.

AMERICAN
IKONE
AMSTERDAM

Brown/Singapore
Blue

① LUST (terms)
→ PROJECTION

↑ RECYCLE OF THE LUST ↓

Theory: when a man is re-born he come out of woman — if he be well not return (ex-cept to experience) exactly why not

* Commonly man's spirit now lives in woman →

MAN is (commonly) IN the woman he projects himself (sees himself out) & thus is a reflection (deflection?) the return trip is the LUST (the urge to return to himself his position inside the woman. Thus most men are consumed — or consume themselves the mortal prisoner of woman

SUN ☉ → SPIRIT — ☽

Process: profunda notations

Low we ... WILL BE DELIBRATE

THE LOGBOOK
OF THE SHIP
"HENRY DAVID THOREAU"

71

DERDE BOEK
YES

WHEN LOVERS BECOME PARENTS

*W*e have just become parents, we hold the helpless newborn infant in our arms and we are overwhelmed by feelings of tenderness towards the tiny being who needs all our protection and nurture, who depends on us completely. We used to be two, now we are three . . .

Lovers who become parents experience a transition in life that results in decisive and irreversible change. The change is evident in many ways – an infant is born and he or she immediately demands our undivided attention round the clock. Soon, our once-tidy home feels cluttered with the infant's many bulky accessories. Furthermore, from the moment of the birth of the child, new and unknown emotions surface within us: instant unconditional love the first time we have eye contact with the child, boundless fear when it falls ill, and genuine despair when we cannot get the child to stop crying. Deep down in our hearts we feel that our child is 100 per cent dependent on us, in a way that no one has ever been before. It may feel somewhat frightening, or perhaps just natural and meaningful. It all depends on what we carry in our baggage from childhood.

Our dependence on one another as a couple also changes when we become parents. Now we are suddenly extremely dependent on each other in completely new ways. Before the child came along, there was no great need for a clear division of labour in the relationship. Now that the child constantly craves our attention, our love relationship also becomes a demanding joint venture. For a great number of good reasons, we will, as parents, encounter emotions and aspects of ourselves of which we were unaware. For this reason, parenthood is a particularly demanding emotional and developmental challenge.

Our everyday life is also changed. Suddenly, a number of activities take some planning or are no longer possible. Gone is the freedom to decide what to do on any normal day; this is now cancelled for the foreseeable future. Just getting out of our house takes a lot of time and energy, and even if we stay at home all the time, more often than not we do not seem to get anything done. It is no longer possible to enjoy an early night with a good book followed by a good night's sleep, or a long candlelit evening with our sweetheart and plenty of red wine.

THE ENORMOUS EXPECTATIONS

In the present time, very powerful expectations and dreams are associated with relationships and family. From the first day of parenthood, the hopeful dreams for "our child" and "our family" put pressure on parents. The tendency is that these hopes and dreams increase in importance with time. More than ever do we want our parenting to be a success, and to have wonderful children who function well and make us proud. This is one of the reasons that a thriving family life is a major indicator of success.

First, there are the expectations of the pregnancy, the birth, and the subsequent stages. Then there will be exterior and interior pressures requiring an ability to handle everything in life while also providing the infant with all the nurture and care he or she needs.

The actual choice of partner and the decision to have children can also contribute to the pressure. These choices are often purely emotional, and we decide autonomously whom we love and with whom we start a family. The free choice of partner offers us the opportunity to make the "right" choice. From a historical perspective, having the freedom to choose the man or woman we want to marry and have children with is only a couple of hundred years old. However, this relatively new situation is not just a gift. Challenges and responsibility for our actions are part of the deal.

In our culture, it is no longer the farm, the social status, or the finances that keep us together. When our relationships are determined only by our choices and feelings, we are faced with considerable demands to develop a strong emotional foundation. Basing our relationships exclusively on our emotions also involves an awareness of the fact that our union may break up because the emotions are no longer present in the right amount, or because our emotional commitment has been diluted with too many unresolved or painful experiences.

Our day and age also presents excessive challenges to parents. Full-time work with the risk of developing stress, a labour market under pressure, an overstretched economy, the constant tyranny of the calendar, and escalating house prices are some of the basic conditions many families with children have to deal with. In addition, we face a great number of typical challenges to the development of close relationships: a working life with variable hours, mobile phones, television, text messages, and mail, which give us the opportunity to stay in touch with the rest of the world. However, this type of communication does not prescribe the nature of our contact, or our presence, which is required to build good relationships.

Changing attitudes regarding the best conditions for children to grow up in may also challenge the parents' relationship. Only a few decades ago, children were not considered independent human beings with their own rights and needs. Many parents who are now above the age of forty-five were raised in the old-fashioned way, where *children were supposed to be seen, but not heard*, and where mothers followed the health visitor's advice about children needing a *calm, quiet, and regulated* environment.

In the 1970s, the views on child rearing changed radically. The key words then were stimulation and raising creative children who were at the centre of things. The prevalent pedagogical attitude was that children were able to take full responsibility for their own learning, that essentially they knew everything, that they had a clear sense of, for instance, when to go to bed and what clothes to wear.

One of the exciting things about our time is that we are in the process of understanding yet another view on childhood. It is based on the assumption that children are not just children who will develop on their own, but that children can only develop in close and confident interaction with significant adults. These adults are responsible for the quality of the framework and the interaction that is created. In other words, we should not do something to the children, but something *with* the children.

Bearing in mind the challenges to parenthood, it is good to know that at the beginning of our career as parents, as in all other major transitions in life, we have a unique opportunity. The transition is a unique opportunity to develop new insights and realizations, new knowledge, strength, vitality, and intimacy. Ever ingenious, nature has devised the law that when we make a transition from one stage in life to the next, we also experience physical changes – for instance, during puberty, pregnancy, and menopause. These changes and the attendant emotions help us take a look at our own internal world. In these phases, the psyche is more open, flexible, and receptive – and also more vulnerable. All things considered, this means that transitions and crises are the best times for gaining new knowledge about ourselves and each other. After such a process, we may emerge with more self-knowledge and an increased ability to create confident and close relationships; in other words, a greater capacity for becoming better parents.

WE WATCH OUR CHILDREN THROUGH A MAGNIFYING GLASS

When the winds of change blow, some people build wind-breakers, others build windmills . . .

The old Chinese saying reminds us that change should be seen as an opportunity for development. Parenthood offers the same prospect of perceiving a challenge as either a threat or an opportunity. When we feel under pressure as a partner or as a parent, we can choose to entrench ourselves in various ways or to open up and see the opportunities the situation offers. When we become parents the question is not if we will encounter these challenges. It is a question of when and how we, as partners and parents, share and tackle these challenges that often involve the experience of dependence, fear, exhaustion, expectation, and joy.

When we, as parents, dare to feel and share our vulnerability and openness, we give ourselves, our partner, and our child optimal opportunities to experience and develop love, closeness, and intimacy. It sounds so simple, but in reality many of us end up not following this path, even if we want the best for our children. The question is, do we realize what wanting the best for our children actually entails? The majority of us choose to create a family on the basis of the hope, the will, and the wish that we will succeed in living together as a family and that it will also be wonderful once we get started. We assume that our love for each other and the wish to create a family is a strong and adequate foundation for a successful, vibrant, confident, and harmonious family with resilient, secure, and balanced children.

However, unfortunately, our parenthood often does not develop the way we had hoped and anticipated. It takes more than love and goodwill to create a vibrant family. All too many families fail to thrive. Instead, we experience quarrels and despair in our daily lives, not knowing what to do and how to move on. It is unbearable to realize that when the family is challenged we, the parents, often tend to look at the children's behaviour through a magnifying glass instead of focusing on our own conduct. The problems a large number of children experience are often symptomatic of underlying issues that preoccupy the significant adults in their lives.

Whether we live in a nuclear family, as single parents, or in a family with children from different marriages, the point of departure is the same: family and children function on the foundation created by the adults. It might be a large pill to swallow that our child's problems are a reflection of the ways in which we ourselves interact with our partner. The fact that it also involves the atmosphere between, and the communication with, ex-husbands and wives, stepmothers and stepfathers, and grandparents does not make the pill easier to swallow. We all breathe the same air and, thereby, also the "pollution" we adults create. Regardless of whether the problem is located in the relationship between the parents, the grandparents and their own adult children, the purpose of this book is the same: how to meet differences, disagreements, and wounded feelings in ways that do not create distance and insecurity; how to relate to challenges in ways that promote understanding and development, as opposed to creating distance, anger, despair, and grief.

We are capable of turning everything upside down and defining the power of parenthood with the words, "What an opportunity for growth and development, what an opportunity to realize my innermost longings and make my dreams of relationship as well as family come true!"

Living in a relationship over time is, in itself, a gigantic challenge. However, becoming a parent for life is an even greater task.

Just like a love affair, a birth is a euphoric landmark event. The new life is a blank page, the beginning of an extraordinary chapter in the book of life. However, once the emotions and the hormonal storms of the body have subsided, our daily routine begins again. We are back to an everyday situation, where day-to-day parenthood gradually takes over. Essentially, our parenthood can develop in one of two directions:

- towards a vibrant long-term couple relationship and parenthood;
- towards a relationship and a family life characterized by endless power struggles and parallel lives - perhaps with a divorce as the only way out.

Why is it so difficult to function as parents? Because once the children come along, particular forces come into play. Before we have children, there may be plenty of room for different positions and changes. We do not find it problematic to let go of issues we do not approve of or live with an unsatisfied longing. However, when we become parents, these different positions become much clearer. It is almost as if these differences are magnified. Suddenly, we discover aspects of our partner we were unaware of and of which we might not approve. Perhaps I see the independent and competent woman I fell in love with become fussy and anxious in her attitude towards the infant. I may find my wonderful, warm, and gentle sweetheart on edge, expressing in no uncertain terms that it cannot be right that a small child of three months should control the entire family night and day. Perhaps I will experience that the closeness and the intimacy with my partner has changed – *we were once so close and now . . .*

When we start a family, we are forced to look at our differences in a new way. All the things we previously accepted – that my lover always slept late on weekends or enjoyed meeting up with colleagues after work – suddenly become unusually difficult to live with. One of the unexpected aspects of life in a relationship is that it is precisely these differences that in time will generate irritation, criticism, or even contempt. For this reason, we spend much precious time attempting to change each other in order to root out the unpleasant emotions generated by our differences.

Do you think you will succeed? Have you tried? In that case, you know that it is an entirely fruitless endeavour to attempt to change your partner if your partner does not wish to change. It is an illusion to think that we are troubled or pleased by the same things, that we can always achieve intimacy on all accounts, that we see the same qualities in our children, that we dream about or expect the same achievements by our children. If, against all the odds, we still attempt to do so, our parenting and our couple relationship end in a place where there is no room for us as the unique people we are. Alternatively, we end up in a situation where we expect that the other person should be able to guess and fulfil our needs and desires.

Becoming a parent involves learning about new aspects of our self and our partner that require a response. We might not have been aware of these aspects before, but now they are present with a vengeance in our daily life, perhaps even with damaging effects. Hence, the great parental challenge is to figure out how we create an intimacy in our lives that embraces our children and our partner when we disagree, while also allowing us to continue to live together as a family. It sounds like a doomsday scenario. However, we would like to point out that this situation contains new, completely different, and attractive opportunities.

The fact is that it is only when we learn to become aware of the opportunities our differences create, tackle them, and discover how to be at ease in this potentially conflictual space, that we can set love free for real and allow intimacy and vitality to flourish.

IF I HAD ONLY KNOWN THAT ABOUT YOU!

Lars and Signe have just become parents. Lars also has a daughter of nine, so he has experience as a parent. Signe is surprised at the intensity of her feelings towards their infant, as previously she was not particularly interested in babies. Hence, it is a very intense experience for her suddenly to hold her own child, whom she loves beyond measure. Nothing in the world matters more than ensuring that the tiny infant gets all the love and nurture she knows it needs. Lars has a demanding and exciting job which preoccupies him a great deal. When he realized that he was going to become a father for the second time, he was both happy and anxious. He was happy because he felt that Signe was the most wonderful woman on earth, but he was also anxious because he was reminded that now he could, in fact, risk losing his family once again. He knows just how painful it is only to see your child every other weekend and every Tuesday after work.

When Lars and Signe fell in love, they fell for completely different aspects in each other. Lars was thrilled by their intimacy and her understanding of him as a man, a father, and a human being. He had never experienced a woman who was as intimately present and vibrant as Signe. However, even if it was wonderful to get attention and be understood, he also felt that now and then she was a little remote. However, other aspects of Signe could also make Lars uneasy. Dust in corners and a messy home did not seem to worry her. Lars therefore spent every Saturday morning putting the house in order, cleaning and washing. When they were expecting the baby, he naturally wondered how these established routines would be affected. However, he was convinced that the child would inspire Signe to impose order on her chaos and clean the corners.

Signe, in turn, was attracted to Lars because he was a "real man" who was confident and had an ordered life with a regular job and goals on many levels. Her other relationships had been with men who did not know what they wanted to do with their lives, so this man came as a godsend.

Lars was 100% engaged in the birth and just as moved as Signe when their little daughter was born. The first weeks were amazing. Even if Signe cried a lot now and then, she felt that they both participated equally in their parenting.

She experienced that Lars was very caring towards her as well as towards the baby.

Two months later, Lars celebrated his birthday, and Signe had bought a beautiful birthday card for him from the baby. The text on the card said: "For the world's best father", and they had decided to invite guests over for a birthday dinner. They were running late, and Lars was a little stressed and concerned that they might not get everything ready by the time the guests arrived. He asked Signe if she could please hurry up with feeding the baby, so that she could come and help him. Then Signe became stressed and the baby cried and would not feed.

Then something happened. Lars got worked up in a way she had never experienced before. He took the crying baby and put her in her cradle seat. In no uncertain terms he told her to sit quietly while they finished cooking the meal. Signe was not just upset; she was beside herself, and cried and told Lars that the child had no way of knowing that they were having guests over for dinner and that it was unfair to stress the child in such a way. Lars responded, now in a louder and even sharper tone of voice, "A baby should not bloody well prevent us from having people over for dinner!"

Signe was in shock. At that moment 10,000 thoughts ran through her mind. She suddenly doubted everything. She doubted her capacities as a mother; she was in doubt about Lars and their future. And again – did he really say that? The way he had spoken to her made her world collapse. She tore up the birthday card.

CRITICISM IS ABOUT LONGING

Criticism, or the feeling of frequently being criticized, feeds the dark side of parenthood. For this reason, we would rather not experience criticism. The energy lodged in our frustrations needs to be used as a stepping stone to free ourselves from the power struggles that wear out so many parents. After many years of running a therapeutic practice for couples, our experience is that if we welcome frustrations into our lives, we will access enormous resources of energy and development. How, then, should we understand this phenomenon?

Imagine that your painful experiences from childhood are like a volcano. They smoulder underground, but this remains hidden from our sight. However, from time to time, the volcano spurts lava from its interior. Whether it is eruptions or just a constant smouldering, the "lava" emerges from us as criticism, frustration, or anger, and it is experienced by our partner as scorn, threats, or humiliation. All the emotional "lava" has one thing in common: it consists of a bedrock of old experiences.

If we can work out what these experiences are all about, we can find nuggets of pure gold in our frustrations. Perhaps they consist of a longing for something we needed as a child but never received, a longing for comfort that never arrived after a frightening event, a longing for understanding of a situation beyond our control that made us unhappy. Gradually, a memory may surface behind our protestations, entrenched positions, or disagreements. At this point, we can piece together the story of what we are being reminded of and begin to deal with it.

When working with frustrations and criticisms, the codeword is longing. The reason is that behind every recurring criticism you find a frustration, and below that lingers a longing in the person who criticizes. The frustration or the criticism is, therefore, not the core issue. The core issue is to understand the underlying longing and what it is that we are being reminded of. We would say that 90% of a criticism or a frustration concerns past experiences of the person who is criticizing or is frustrated. Only 10% has to do with what our partner does or does not do!

This understanding is essential. Our criticism might be a strong factor that freezes our partner in precisely the behaviours we wish he or she would be able to move away from. By learning to express the longing embedded in a criticism, we can transform power struggles into productive learning experiences.

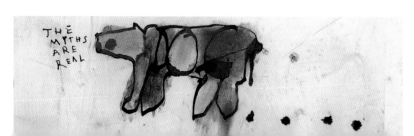

WHERE IS THE MAN I ONCE FELL IN LOVE WITH?

May has a profound longing for lots of spontaneity and laughter in her little family with her husband Christian and their child Thea, aged three. The reason for this longing is that she comes from an undemonstrative family where fun and games and expressions of joy were rare. Instead of expressing her longing, she often takes out her frustrations on her husband, expressing the frustrations and not the longings: "Why don't you surprise me more? Sometimes it all gets a little too drab and predictable!" "Why can't you just sit down and laugh a little at *Bananas in Pyjamas* with Thea. That programme is actually quite funny!" May ends up criticizing and blaming Christian and their family life. She criticizes the fact that they never do anything spontaneously and that they cannot laugh at the same things. She might also be angered by the fact that there is too much telling-off in their little family. This is actually rather strange, because before they had their child, Christian was actually very amusing. Where are all the fun times now? Sometimes May is even in doubt about whether or not Christian is the right man for her.

THE BATTLE TO BE RIGHT

Consensus in the world of research shows that the people who succeed in having good relationships and families tend not to allow differences, disagreements, and criticism to lead to endless power struggles about being right. These power struggles always lead to more dogfights, more silence, more insecure and stressed children, less intimacy, less joy, less laughter, fun, and games.

We are all familiar with the daily exchanges of opinions where we are quickly caught up in a disagreement, often focusing more on that than on what we actually want to say to each other. We can become so preoccupied with the discussion about being right that we lose focus on the joint venture that is the basis of our life together as parents. In the heat of the argument we tend to forget that we create neither more intimacy or contact nor a good atmosphere by being right. On the contrary! Nevertheless, that is often our focus: being right about how we would like to influence and raise our children, how the family should live, what rules and attitudes are important.

Some examples might be:

"She must learn to have her teeth brushed without screaming and shouting."
Yes, that would be wonderful, but she will not be motivated to do so when you hold her tight and force her to open her mouth.

"He must know that when we say that he should go to bed, then he should do so."
Oh, I think it is all right that we are not so strict about bedtime during weekends. He is old enough to understand that.

"She should not be allowed to leave the table before the rest of us have finished our meals . . ."
Well, you cannot expect that a child of that age will understand that . . .

We imagine that we can convince our partner that our way of brushing teeth, etc., is the best. But that is the same as believing that we can tame a lion by addressing it politely. It is not that easy – and we do not convince our partner about anything by saying it in a louder voice. When we talk about how to raise our children, we are indirectly talking about our own childhood experiences as if they were the truth. This is how we process all the other longings that our partner is unaware of.

OLD BEHAVIOUR PATTERNS DRIVE OUR SURVIVAL STRATEGIES

It is quite human that frustrations, criticism, and blame can be our first reaction when we are not on top of things. When unpleasant emotions and conflicts loom large on the horizon, our survival mechanisms are activated. Survival mechanisms are deeply personal patterns for tackling major, difficult, and painful challenges. These mechanisms were formed in our childhood as a necessary shield for us to get on in a demanding and complex world. The mechanisms would, for instance, help us to speak up, become angry and sad. However, the unproductive aspect of our survival strategies is that they can be activated unconsciously for the rest of our lives every time we encounter an emotional challenge, feel threatened, criticized, or afraid.

As a parent this might, for instance, be when we experience:

- that our partner tells off our child in a severe way, so that our child is sad and frightened;
- that our partner does not respond, even if we express a need for intimacy and closeness;
- that our partner questions our way of being a parent.

First, we feel insecure, but then we begin to defend or entrench ourselves in the survival strategies we developed as children. Essentially, we apply the same simple survival strategies as those used in the animal kingdom:

- the flight reaction;
- the fight reaction;
- the freeze reaction.

THE FLIGHT REACTION

As human beings, we are more developed than animals. Hence, we also have more sophisticated ways of expressing our survival strategies. This does not mean that flight necessarily manifests itself in storming out of the house screaming at the top of our lungs. The flight strategy can also be to stay on after work socializing with colleagues, or to sit in front of the computer or the television, or to go out of our way to avoid conflict situations.

Sometimes my wife is not satisfied with the way I behave. I get upset when she gets so angry and all worked up. When I listen to her reproaches, I feel so helpless and exhausted that I finally get up and leave. Either I say that the dog needs to be taken for a walk or that I am going for a run . . . then I hope that she will be in a better mood when I return.

THE FIGHT REACTION

The fight reaction can be much more than a physical attack. Scolding, criticizing, or blaming are other non-physical ways of attacking. The moment we say "You always . . ." or "You never . . .", we are actually in the process of attacking and most probably we will be met with a counter attack: "What about yourself . . ."

My husband sometimes thinks that I am too soft towards our son. He thinks I should restrain our son more. I find this very provocative and when Jonathan has been put to bed and we discuss this, I sometimes lose my temper and give him the full treatment . . . saying that a child would not learn anything from his need to play the dictator. I get furious and sad, and when I defend my son, I often do not know when to stop.

THE FREEZE REACTION

To freeze can mean that we experience a momentary psychological paralysis, put everything on hold, and try to be as unreceptive and invisible as possible. Our emotions and reactions are "frozen" until the danger has passed. Think of the rabbit that suddenly lies completely immobile when it feels threatened. For a human being, the freeze survival strategy works like putting on a protective suit that prevents us from reacting to or feeling anything.

My otherwise gentle girlfriend sometimes blows her top at my way of raising our children. She can become very aggressive. In those situations I am almost afraid of her, and all kinds of thoughts go through my head. However, I get completely paralysed and have no idea what to say or do to stop her. I feel powerless and withdraw into myself emotionally.

What all survival strategies have in common is that they are counteracting the openness, the intimacy, and the closeness which are the building blocks of any vibrant relationship and family. For this reason, it is a considerable advantage for us as lovers, parents, or friends to gain knowledge about the nature of the survival strategies we carry in our baggage. Knowledge about how to disengage from them is particularly useful. When we are able to let go of the survival strategies, we automatically avoid the scenarios in which they come between us and our loved ones, and we avoid passing them on to our children.

LONELINESS WHEN TOGETHER

If we end up attacking and criticizing each other, being cold and distant and lacking in confidence, it becomes difficult to be together. Often, we have no idea whatsoever about what to do to get out of a pattern that, deep in our hearts, we know leads to a dead end. What do we do when we experience that we cannot reconcile our differences and power struggles? What do we do when we cannot accept the other person, or when we do not feel understood by our partner? Often, the result is that the futile quarrels about child rearing and relationships do not serve any purpose. On the contrary! When we realize that we cannot change our partner, the distance between us substantially increases. What used to be a small rift may, in time, begin to look like an ever-widening abyss. If we begin to withdraw from our partner because we are giving up trying to be understood, we may automatically turn to our child. Of course, we have been there for our child all along, but if our needs for contact and intimacy with our partner are not met, we attempt to fulfil those needs with our child. In this way, a vibrant family life becomes ever more elusive as still more areas of our family life are split up into parallel lives (e.g., with the mother and the child on one side, and the father on the other side). The couple relationship, their sex life, and shared parenthood are gradually put on standby. In time, the child gets used to this division, where it is "normal" that only one parent participates in various activities in and outside the home.

YET ANOTHER COOL EVENING . . .

The dinner is over and Jan walks to and from the kitchen sink and the table. Five-year-old Lise stands on her chair and begins to jump. Jan's wife Hanne notices, and smiles and nods to Lise that it is OK. It warms her heart to see that Lise is enthusiastic and spontaneous. She has missed seeing Lise happy lately. However, Jan does not see this. Instead, he tells Lise that she should sit down instead of jumping on the chair. Hanne interrupts him and says, "But she is just dancing!"

Jan is overcome by a sudden irritation and anger – not because Lise jumps on the chair – but because Hanne interrupts and reprimands him in front of the children. He feels that in this way she destroys his effort to teach the children some table manners. For a brief moment, he questions whether he was right in trying to get Lise to sit down.

Hanne also becomes sad. She sees that Lise is frightened and confused – she had just been allowed to jump on the chair and then she was told to sit down. Hanne also feels how the pleasure she takes in Lise's spontaneous happiness disappears in a split second. She thinks that Jan will probably never learn to understand and accept her way of being a mother. Perhaps she is even a bad mother, and what about Lise? She will, no doubt, be influenced by her parents' disagreements about her upbringing. However, Hanne does not want any more conflict in front of Lise, so she defuses the situation by saying that she will tuck Lise in. Jan does not want to quarrel either while Lise is awake, but he also feels that neither he nor Hanne will have the energy to discuss it later. He will probably end up working a little. And then the day will be over. Maybe they will manage to say goodnight, but it will probably be one of those many cool goodnights . . .

Jan's and Hanne's story tells us about typical thoughts and reactions when we feel we are sabotaged as a parent by our partner. If Jan and Hanne do not tell each other about their experiences of the situation, but merely continue to do what they normally do, this little episode will be added to all the other little episodes characterized by the feeling of being misunderstood. And for every additional small episode, yet another brick will be added to the wall of disagreement and old survival strategies between the couple.

At this stage, many couples see a divorce as the only solution. However, even if a divorce might seem to be the only way out of a relationship, it is usually neither easy nor a relief. Beginning a new life as single parents or starting a new family is quite a challenge. We might also form a family where there are children from several marriages and different backgrounds. The choices we make when we start a new family will be affected by our previous experiences in dealing with loss and stress. However, the dilemmas, disagreements, and hurt the couple has experienced prior to the divorce may continue to thrive, still going strong not just in the old relationship, but also in the subsequent relationships. When the misunderstandings accumulate, as in Jan's and Hanne's case, the reasons can be traced to the same cause: the fact that when we are under pressure, our emotions run the show. These ways of reacting originate in our childhood. These sources of stress will remain more or less unchanged regardless of the type of relationship we are in. The central challenge is how to create a sense of security in our own and our partner's lives, so that the entire family feels at ease even when we disagree and our differences are visible in a variety of ways.

THE FAMILY SPIRAL

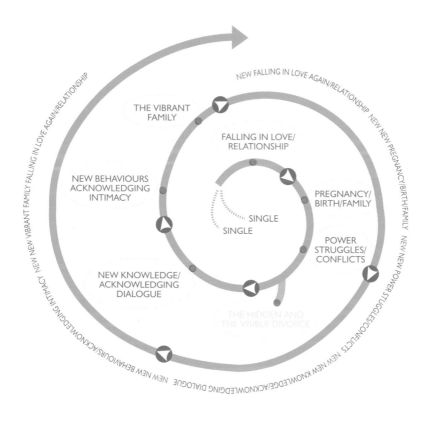

The family's development from the usual to the possible patterns: from the time the relationship begins through the "natural" phases of falling in love, birth of one or more children, power struggles that lead to the "new" stages of understanding, dialogue, acknowledgement, intimacy, and new ways of behaving in the vibrant family. The spiral of development continues into new stages when we fall in love again with the same partner, possibly having more children and managing other less demanding conflicts, and reaching stages where the quality of life increases for the entire family.

DIVORCE OR DEVELOPMENT?

Our responses to the challenges of parenthood vary. We can choose from the following.

1. THE INVISIBLE DIVORCE

We stay together for the sake of the children, and live with distance and conflicts between us. We get the best out of the situation, possibly including parallel lives, distance, and continual quarrels about the same issues interspersed with the occasional friendly encounter. Many couples opt for this solution because it avoids the major issue of a visible, conscious decision to get a divorce. We just continue doing what we have done for many years. The disadvantage of this model is that we can delude ourselves into thinking that living like this will not have a major influence on the way our children thrive or develop. As parents, we often seem to think that disagreements only involve and concern us. We are unable to imagine that the child participates in this "drama". It is alarmingly naïve to think that *he or she is not aware of our conflicts, because we only quarrel when he is asleep.* Or *he or she is so young; he or she does not understand what we are talking about.* We are often incapable of realizing that this is not true, and we do not know what to do about it. Children register the nature of the emotional atmosphere, even if they are unable to express what they are feeling in words.

2. THE VISIBLE DIVORCE

We throw in the towel, give up, and go our separate ways. It turns out to be very difficult to keep any good feelings for each other alive. Moreover, so much wounding criticism and distancing now characterize our life together, so that it is difficult to move on. Often, we do not go ahead with the divorce until one of the partners finds a new love. To many couples, dissolving a family just because we cannot work out how to communicate or because we have fallen out of love seems like an unacceptable admission of failure.

3. WE USE PARENTHOOD AS A UNIQUE OPPORTUNITY FOR DEVELOPMENT

The road to the creation of a vibrant family is paved with a range of fantastic opportunities for development. The majority of all parents long for more intimacy, greater freedom, and a better quality of life. The good news is that this is not wishful thinking. It is possible to accomplish these changes.

A frustration is an expression of a hope or a dream that something could be different. Our experience as therapists is based on long careers in therapeutic fields focusing on couples and families with children. In our minds, there is no doubt that a sustained effort to create acknowledging intimacy is the answer to how we can transform frustrated and stressed children and adults discontented with their lives into a vibrant family. We have also seen an endless number of wonderful examples of how parenthood is a unique chance for us as a couple to develop ourselves, our relationship, and our parenthood together. In other words, parenthood is a fantastic opportunity to turn our innermost longings and dreams of relationship as well as family into reality!

A VIBRANT CONFIDENT FAMILY LOOKS LIKE THIS

The adults accept the responsibility for the creation of a good and confident emotional atmosphere between the two of them and in the home

The adults show respect for one another, together as well as when with their children

The adults accept and tackle differences, together as well as when with their children

The adults co-operate and support each other

The adults re-establish connection and intimacy after times of conflicts, stress, insecurity, silence, etc., together as well as when with their children

Children and parents feel free and confident to express themselves

---

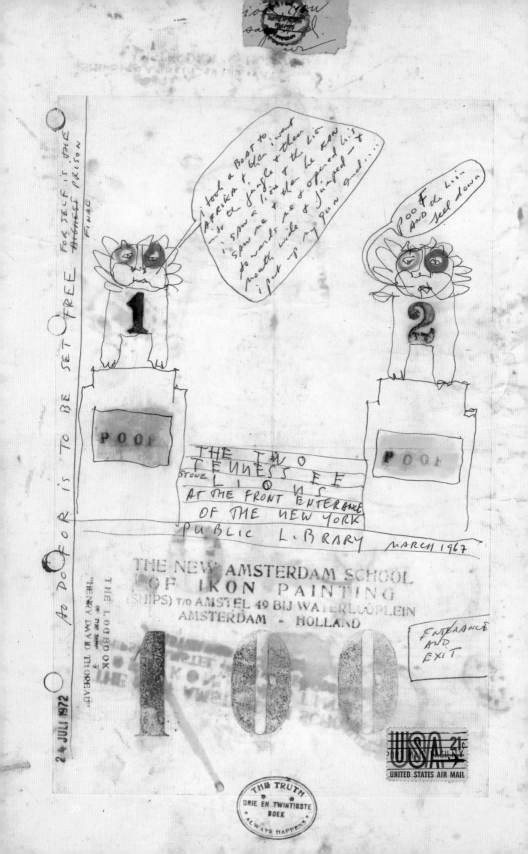

ATTACHMENT AND EXPLORATION IN FOCUS

C hildren have two essential central psychological needs that can only be met through interaction with their parents or caregivers:

- attachment to significant adults;
- exploration of their environment.

As parents, one of our most important tasks is to ensure that our children are able to seek comfort and nurture from us when they are sad, confused, and exhausted, and dare to go exploring, be it in the strawberry bed, the forest, or at school.

In simpler terms, one could say that our children develop on the basis of two kinds of behaviour:

- they seek intimacy and contact (attachment behaviour);
- they explore the world (exploratory behaviour).

Normally, these two apparently opposite types of behaviour do not occur at the same time. Attachment behaviour can be caused by malaise, anxiety, pain, unpredictability, and insecurity, while exploratory behaviour comes from feeling safe and secure, from feeling confidence, warmth, predictability, and reliability. Together with the care-giving adult, the child develops an ability to tolerate appropriate levels of frustration as he or she alternates between these two types of behaviour.

The central foundation point of a child's attachment pattern, as well as his or her exploratory pattern, is the safe and secure base with his or her parents. For this reason, one of our most important tasks as parents is to create a stable lifestyle. This is a central precondition for the child's development of enough self-esteem, self-confidence, and independence, traits that will enable him or her to create and maintain friendships and emotionally close relationships.

When we offer the child acknowledging intimacy, we create a secure base. We do so by providing the child with an assurance that we are available for when he or she needs us as well as allowing ourselves to be seen with our unique personalities and characteristics. The more confidence the child experiences, the greater will be its appetite for exploring the world.

It is important to stress that isolated incidents of insecurity do not undermine the child's store of self-confidence. The creation of the child's personality is best understood as a long journey of emotional development to maturity, the personality growing out of the many repetitive situations and experiences encountered.

Psychologists usually talk about developing either a secure or an insecure attachment pattern, which can be seen in adults as well as children, when we interact with other people. Our attachment pattern is a way of existing in the world. It is not a pattern we notice as such, because it is quickly embedded in our personality. However, it is a determining factor in the formation of our personality, as it begins to be formed at birth.

Unfortunately, only about 60% of children grow up developing a secure attachment pattern. Thirty-five per cent develop one or other of the insecure attachment patterns, while about 5% develop a disorganized attachment pattern. These last two groups – 40% of children – may experience lifelong difficulties in handling life's many emotional challenges and stressful situations. In our roles as parents, we can, therefore, never pay enough attention to the quality of the attachment formed between us and our children. Not only when they are infants, but during the entire time we have the opportunity to nourish a good attachment relationship between us and them.

How do we support the development of a well-functioning and happy infant? Try to imagine that all the things which he or she is, and will eventually become, will grow out of close relationships. The infant cannot, of his or her own accord, create enthusiasm, contentment, or independence, just as he or she cannot generate sadness or anger. Only in his or her exchange with adults and by being mirrored by adults will the infant gradually begin to develop an identity with a full range of senses. If the infant is met with acceptance, he or she will experience a full sense of identity and gradually begin to learn what to do in order to make contact, feel security, and experience love.

Knowledge of our attachment patterns can make it easier to understand some of the reactions we experience with our children and in the interaction with our partners. In addition, this knowledge provides an understanding of the need for patience: even when we decide to do something other than what we normally do, we find we are up against persistent old habits of behaviour.

There is a clear connection between parental attachment patterns and the attachment patterns children develop. This means that when we, as parents gradually change our own attachment patterns and the interaction with our partner changes, our child's attachment pattern will also change. There is no better argument for working on any of our own adult insecure attachment patterns.

ATTACHMENT OCCURS AT AN EARLY STAGE

As parents, the attachment pattern we have carried forward from our own childhood and youth is expressed in relation to our child even before it is born. During pregnancy, we protect the child by, for instance, eating healthy foods and avoiding tobacco and alcohol. During this stage, the mother experiences changes in her sense of self that give her a better capacity to feel empathy and sympathy towards the needs of the child. We have plenty of thoughts and ideas of what kind of a child it will be. "I think he will be a footballer, just like his father. He is already very active," we say, and imagine a little boy in dirty football shorts. We read books, attend antenatal classes, and share the joy of the interaction with the child in reality and in the imagination. "Now she is kicking away . . . try to feel my tummy." *I wonder if she will inherit your temper, or be quiet in the mornings like me?*

All the ideas we parents have of the child are part and parcel of the development of parenthood. From being wanted and imagined, the child becomes real to us the day it is born. The psychological preparation for parenthood centres our contact with the infant from the minute it arrives. However, we are not the only ones preparing. The child is also in the process of getting used to us. We do not understand precisely what the unborn infant senses, but we do know that a newborn infant is capable of distinguishing the parents' voices from other voices because he or she is already accustomed to them.

It is a most special life event to share the experience of the moment when the infant is born. We simply cannot take our eyes off the little miracle. A newborn infant has an innate drive to seek contact with us when we nurture him or her. He or she will, among other things, attempt to respond to eye contact and imitate the movements of our lips and our facial expressions. Here, the infant demonstrates attachment behaviour by calling out to us, crying or making other sounds as soon as it experiences "danger", which is when he or she feels hungry, tired, cold, or alone and in need of contact. All this is part of the child's biological inheritance. As parents, we respond with nurture to these attempts at making contact. If we repeatedly show in both verbal and non-verbal ways that we will always be sympathetic to the child's needs, he or she will, over time, experience that the world is a safe and good place to be. Parents are the first people to perform this function; later, more significant others come along, and in this way the attachment pattern develops very quickly during the first three years. By the age of twelve, the basic features of the attachment pattern are in place.

THE ABILITY TO MATCH AND REGULATE EMOTIONS IS A CORNERSTONE OF FEELING SECURE

Children need parental guidance as they learn how to regulate emotions, sleep patterns, hunger, etc. Hence, it is important that we are able to read our children's signals, that we respond to them and match them. Creating a suitable match for the child emotionally and physically means doing neither too much nor too little. Matching is a very important part of parenting, because it builds confidence.

When we match children, we use our senses to see, hear, and feel them. This prompts us to provide the response which our children's behaviour calls for. At the same time, we need to put our own unsettled and inappropriate emotions for the situation on hold. Otherwise, we easily do "too much" or "too little" and do not offer our child the response he or she needs. Perhaps a tired four-year-old needs to rest for a while on our lap to calm down, or our teenager who has just split up with a sweetheart needs a comforting arm round his or her shoulder and a peaceful moment with a cup of tea. Combined with the emotional matching, the physical contact creates the sense of security that makes the child or the adolescent feel all right, grounded, and able to express the emotions he or she needs to share.

We begin to match our child from day one. For instance, when the infant smiles at us we want to imitate the smile, and exaggerate our facial expression so that he or she realizes that we are responding attentively. Since an infant at that age has a short attention span, we help him or her physically by the way we use our voice. By speaking in a calm, loving tone in a high frequency while maintaining eye contact, we extend the child's attention and physical relaxation for a little longer than the usual attention span. Through this physical matching, the child begins to develop his or her own capacity for matching and empathy.

Another example of matching is the way we respond to the child's attachment behaviour, when we pick up the crying child and comfort him or her. Even if we do not imitate the child's emotions, he or she will, over time, learn that our response in that situation is related to the emotion being expressed by his or her behaviour. The fact that we have a secure and mutual emotional bond develops the child's experience of belonging. Little by little, the child will develop a sense of self and be able to rest confidently in his or her emotions, while at the same time reaching out.

Matching can also be expressed in purely verbal terms, by telling the child what we see: "You are annoyed and sad. Come, let me help you . . ."

When we do not match our children's emotions, we give our children the impression that it is not all right, for instance, to be sad or angry, or that everything is much worse than it perhaps is. If we are not available when our children need us, they will learn that it does not matter to us how they feel and that they must handle their strong emotions alone.

MIRRORING IS GOLD

Another way of matching is through conversation. Matching with words is also called mirroring, and it is increasingly used as a way of clarifying communication. From the parent's point of view, there is instant feedback when we mirror our child's acute emotional condition in a precise and natural way. By mirroring what our child says, we make it clear to him or her that we understand what is at stake so the child has the experience of not being alone. One of the effects of mirroring is that we make our child's seemingly relentless anger or intolerable disappointment visible to him or her. We can also use mirroring in positive situations, because it gives the child the opportunity to enjoy its own success.

A SELF-CONFIDENCE BOOST

Tobias comes home from school and he is very proud. He had only three errors in dictation, which is not his best subject.

Mother mirrors: *You are very proud that you had only three errors in your dictation today!*

In this way, Tobias has the chance to stop and feel that, in fact, he did quite well today: *I had only three spelling mistakes in dictation today. I am really proud of myself.* The self-respect account is boosted immediately.

If, instead, mother had answered, *You are such a clever boy!*, her enthusiasm would not have had the same effect on her son's self-respect. When it is the parent praising the child, the child could become dependent on the parent's evaluation, which is different from developing his or her self-respect.

Mirroring has a lot of beautiful qualities:

- it places the child's or the adult's speech in the full spotlight;

- it increases the opportunity of gaining an in-depth understanding of what the child or the partner says and needs;

- it moves the focus from a problem orientation to an energy orientation, because the child or partner becomes an active player in the conversation and the solution of the problem;

- it reduces the risk of disagreement and conflict;

- it prevents us from wondering about what our next move should be;

- it prevents us from interpreting, responding with disappointment or anxiety, or offering good advice, which may silence further conversation.

MIRRORING IN INFANTS – LOOK WE ARE TALKING!

Sanne and Tim are in the baby-changing room in the maternity ward with their newborn daughter. He attempts to get the diaper to fit the girl. "It will be fun when we can begin to talk with her in about a year," says Tim. "She is already talking a little – in her own way," says Sanne. "Yesterday I got her to imitate me when I stuck my tongue out at her. Try it yourself." Tim leans towards the girl until his face is 25–30 cm from hers. He senses that this is the distance she prefers. He sticks out his tongue and waits a while. Then the girl looks at him and sticks out her tiny tongue. Tim is very moved and tears come to his eyes. "How extraordinary! We are talking, my darling," he says calmly to the baby.

In this way, we can explore different ways of communicating and get to know our child. What makes this momentary contact decisive is that it is associated with an overwhelming feeling of joy and happiness which is felt throughout the body. No wonder that we occasionally feel completely in love with our young child. Sharing this experience and experiencing our partner in a positive interaction with the child brings us closer together as parents and as a couple.

MIRROR NEURONS

The location of the mirror neurons in the human brain is an important new discovery that helps us to understand empathy, which is what we experience when we say, "I am able to feel what you feel". All "mirroring" phenomena – whether we copy our infants' facial expressions and they mirror ours, whether we mirror our children's agitated feelings or mirror our partner in an Acknowledging Dialogue – are, in neuropsychology, called spontaneous, intuitive understanding. This knowledge helps us to understand why mirroring stimulates young children's brains to such a great extent. In addition, the mirroring process also helps us understand why mirroring can continue to be a beneficial activity throughout our lives. The mirror neurons enable us to feel other people's emotions and sense their intentions. This process begins with "intuitions" or sensations, which then graduate to a more conscious, and clear, understanding.

DISCOVERY OF THE MIRROR NEURONS

This is the story of an incidental and extremely important discovery in a centre for brain research in Parma, in Italy. Here, some scientists were doing research into the development and function of monkey brains, right down to cell level. During a break, a member of the research team was eating peanuts. In the same room, there was a monkey whose brain was still wired up to the electrodes connected to the individual cells, which in previous experiments had initiated the act of "eating peanuts". By chance, one of the scientists noticed a synchronicity between his rustling of paper and chewing of peanuts, and brain activity in the cage a few feet away, where the monkey was listening and watching. However, the monitor registered amplitude levels identical to those produced when the monkey ate the peanuts. He concluded that the wish to eat peanuts was set off in the monkey's brain, but not the act in itself.

The experiment was expanded to include the sound of eating peanuts, but not the sight. The same result occurred. What was discovered by coincidence could be understood as the monkey's mental processing of what the researcher did. A kind of resonance occurred, an accurate mirroring of sense impressions. The cells that have this critical function are called mirror cells, or mirror neurons.

WHAT DOES AN ATTACHMENT PATTERN LOOK LIKE?

Our knowledge of children's attachment patterns stems from the comprehensive research into attachment undertaken and developed through the past fifty years. Research is often carried out in a classical situation, where a child is partly observed with a mother, partly with a stranger, and partly alone. All experiments take place in the span of minutes. The child's reactions when the mother leaves and returns are observed and described.

Research demonstrates that the attachment pattern is found in all cultures worldwide, and it also shows that children of parents with different attachment patterns adapt varying attachment patterns for each parent. Hence, we have not only one attachment pattern, but a variety of them in our baggage.

We invite you to read about attachment patterns with curiosity and use the ideas with respect and care. This book is meant as an appetizer and an introduction to a new discovery, not as a criticism of your child, your partner, or yourself.

THE SECURELY ATTACHED CHILDREN

The securely attached child will, during childhood, experience many interactions where he or she feels met, seen, respected, and loved. This means that a child learns to appreciate and to commit to close relationships without fear of being abandoned. The approximately 60% of children who are securely attached also develop an ability to regulate strong feelings and stressful situations without being overwhelmed. These children also develop an ability to see others as individuals, with separate emotions and intentions, which they acknowledge and respect. This means that a child develops a fundamental acknowledging attitude to its fellow human beings. All these excellent skills are not inborn bonuses, but a product of the parents' ability to create a secure base.

Typically, the parents of securely attached children are sensitive, accepting, co-operative, predictable, attentive, and accessible. These parents express a realistic but positive view of the child and themselves, and focus on the child's life as well as their own adult lives.

Securely attached children seem content, play games, and seek contact when they need comfort. Hence, they develop flexibility and empathy, and when they feel rejected they respond robustly.

An example: *Your child falls and gets hurt, cries, and runs towards you. You comfort your child, hold him or her close, and say that you understand how much it hurts. When your child shows you that he or she is ready, you let go, and he or she returns to a new round of games.*

CHILDREN ARE YOURS FOREVER

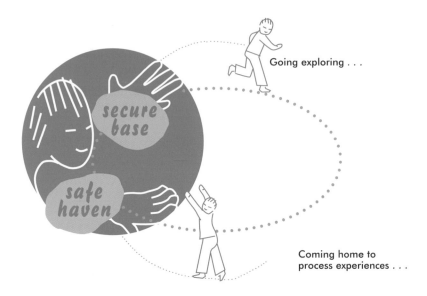

Going exploring . . .

Coming home to
process experiences . . .

The circle of attachment describes what it takes to create a secure attachment. The child who experiences a secure base, where both parents are present in a close, predictable, stable, and attentive way, will dare to explore a still greater world because he or she knows there will always be a safe harbour to return to. This is not so different from the adult situation when we explore and challenge ourselves in the world! However, doing so with a safe harbour behind us makes a world of difference. Precisely the same process unfolds in the couple relationship and in parenthood. Children and adults who feel safe and secure will have an easier time matching other people's feelings and regulating their own feelings.

(Inspired by *The Circle of Security* by Glen Cooper, Kent Hoffman, Robert Marvin, and Bert Powell.)

THE INSECURELY ATTACHED CHILDREN

There are two kinds of insecure attachment patterns:

- the insecurely attached child with dismissive behaviour (approximately 20%);
- the insecurely attached child with anxious behaviour (approximately 15%).

THE INSECURELY ATTACHED CHILD – WITH DISMISSIVE BEHAVIOUR

The insecurely attached child experiences an unsatisfied need for predictable contact and attention. Hence, it will not behave like children with secure attachment patterns, who engage in games, learning, and exploration of the world. This child's development is limited because of its unmet need for secure attachment. The child's vital energy is influenced by its need for protection, because it often experiences being rejected, overlooked, or misunderstood. For this reason, the child learns to defend itself against rejection and feelings of being abandoned. This child may, for instance, refrain from seeking comfort when he or she feels insecure or afraid. This child may also refrain from showing his or her own needs and instead focus on toys or other things. Children with an insecure attachment pattern characterized by dismissive behaviour show little awareness of their own or other people's feelings. They have lots of language, but a limited vocabulary when they tell their own stories, called their autobiographical story or narrative. They have problems finding inner calm and are susceptible to stress.

Insecurely attached children with dismissive behaviour show only a few external signs of sadness when their mother leaves. They tend to be more tense and inhibited when they play. They spend all their energy in coping.

Parents of children with this type of attachment pattern are often dismissive and show unpredictable levels of attention. They tend to distance themselves physically by offering activities to the child instead of close contact. Because of the child's insecurity, he or she has low expectations of other people, and so he or she is often rejected. This child does not get the love he or she needs, does not experience being deserving of love, attempts to live without love and support, becomes evasive, and, thus, again often experiences rejection.

In summary, we would say that these children, when in critical and stressful situations, will tend to act without being in touch with their feelings or without expressing their feelings. An example: *Your child falls and is hurt. He or she does not run to you for comfort. Instead, he or she quickly begins a new activity. You let it pass.*

THE INSECURELY ATTACHED CHILD – WITH ANXIOUS BEHAVIOUR

These children constantly crave attention. They seek contact, but alternate between clinging and dismissive behaviour. Their playing is inhibited, and so they often sit passively by, watching without facial expressions. Adults' attempts at engaging them in games can be met with anger.

This attachment pattern occurs in an interaction where mother and father are available to the child in an unpredictable way. In some situations, mother and father will be available and accommodating towards the child. In other situations, they are beyond the child's reach. This unpredictability might be due to the fact that the parents spend a lot of time away from home. It may also be due to stress, psychological instability, or illness, which again results in unreliable contact and closeness. Insecurely attached children with anxious behaviour often become very sad when their mother leaves. When she returns, they are difficult to calm down or comfort.

Parents with this type of attachment pattern are often less responsive and unpredictably attentive to their children's expressions of anger and frustration. They are often characterized by a deep anxiety for their child, and relate in inconsequential ways. Sometimes, they pay too much attention, and at other times, too little attention, to their child.

On a daily basis, the experience of their child's needs often comes first, and they put their other roles in life on hold while trying to meet their child's needs, thereby reinforcing the children's dependence on them. One could say that these children and parents, in critical and stressful situations, are overwhelmed by emotions to the extent that they are almost incapable of knowing what action to take.

An example: *Your child falls and is hurt, cries a lot, and runs to you for comfort. You are already on tenterhooks. Frightened and agitated, you get up and run to meet the child. You pick up the child and give him or her lots of comfort for a long time. You experience that the child needs you to go on giving comfort and you stay with the child.*

THE CHILD WITH DISORGANIZED ATTACHMENT

A small group of children (approximately 5%) are characterized by an extremely disturbed attachment pattern. This pattern is seen in children who have grown up under very difficult circumstances. Their parents' childhood was characterized by stressful experiences to the extent that they are incapable of reading their own children's needs for security and contact. These parents respond with irritation, aggression, or anxiety when their child cries or is experienced as demanding. In some cases, this may lead to psychological or physical parental violence. The result is that the children become afraid of the parents' reactions on the one hand, while also instinctively attempting to bond with them. Being confronted with such an impossible task leads to many serious attachment disturbances in the child, who will be very unpredictable, at odds with him- or herself, and lack inner calm. Due to the inner chaos, he or she shuttles to and fro in no-man's-land.

MASTERY OR SURVIVAL

From birth onwards, the child will experience mastery and/or survival. One example could be the area of food, where the infant may feel hunger and express his or her need for food. Whether or not his or her hunger will be satisfied depends on the parents' response. If the infant predominantly experiences that, by and large, his needs are satisfied, then he will have an easier time enduring waiting and frustration. If there is a reliable parent in the child's vicinity, who can help him regulate his feelings, the child will "borrow" some of the adult's calm and so gradually learn to create and maintain his own calm and balance. Hence, the children who have experienced, at an early age, that it helps to express yourself, will seek help and have an easier time learning to solve problems. These children develop strategies for mastering complex situations. Children's survival strategies are focused on finding ways to protect themselves against experiencing anxiety, pain, and loneliness. Survival strategies are the classical "fight, flight, or freeze" reactions, so that the children show either disproportionately violent or defeatist and apathetic behaviour.

Hence, it is always important not to blame children for their strategies for survival and insecure patterns of behaviour. Blaming will only reinforce these strategies and increase the distance to mastery of self and life. The quality of the nurture and the contact with which we engage with our children will be significant in terms of whether the exploratory behaviour or the attachment behaviour will dominate and determine which strategies of mastery and survival the child will develop to deal with the challenges of life.

In a larger perspective, the way in which we respond to our children's behaviours will determine whether or not they have confidence in the surrounding world and dare to explore it.

In summary, we would say that the development of a specific attachment pattern will inform the balance in our lives between:

- mastery strategies, where the child learns appropriate ways to get attention, security, nurture, closeness, or physical contact;

and

- survival strategies, where the child develops methods to avoid the pain of not getting attention, security, nurture, closeness, or physical contact.

6 9

Now

FRIENDS AND ENEMIES

I. it is popular to say suppose it
is important who ones friends
are (who are your friends? then
know who you are)

II. but it may be more important
who ones Enemies are
(who are your enemies? then
i know you)

SECURE CHILDREN DEVELOP A GREATER DEGREE OF MASTERY

When young children begin to feel secure, they need to explore the surrounding world and attempt to do things on their own. The parents follow their children with vigilant eyes, ready to step in if they should encounter problems. It is as if there is an invisible connection, and the moment the child is in danger, parent and child will be reunited and feel secure again.

The child who experiences a secure base where the parents are close in predictable, stable, and attentive ways will dare to explore an even greater part of the surrounding world. The reason is that the child trusts that a safe harbour will always await him or her with the parents. Hence, a secure child is more daring, will acquire more problem-solving skills, and experience the world. The accumulation of positive experiences has a reinforcing effect. When a child experiences mastery in life, he or she develops a firm foundation of his or her belief in the ability to handle minor and major challenges in life.

INSECURE CHILDREN DEVELOP MORE SURVIVAL STRATEGIES

All insecurely attached children experience that powerlessness and despair often lead to the development of survival strategies. These children do not develop the skills of mastery that we see in securely attached children.

As a matter of course, insecurely attached children are not nearly as interested in conquering the world and trying out the many options life has to offer. They are inhibited by a feeling of being just able to handle their life in the here and now. This factor contributes significantly to their tendency to let the opportunities for discovery pass by.

ADULT ATTACHMENT PATTERNS

All our childhood attachment experiences form the basis for the patterns of behaviour we can expect from the people who are near to us, and on whom we depend. If we have developed a secure attachment pattern in our childhood, it will be easier for us as adults to listen to and contain other people's feelings and regulate our own. Hence, couples who both have secure attachment patterns are in a better position to maintain or restore the acknowledging intimacy when they hurt each other, or when problems mount up.

However, for couples in which one or both have insecure attachment patterns because of having grown up without sufficient reliability and attentiveness from their parents, the situation is different. When these couples have conflicts, or feel a lack of mutual respect or recognition, it is not easy to restore acknowledging intimacy. These couples' survival strategies can control their interaction full time. If our desire is not met, a survival strategy may be activated in the hope of regaining more intimacy. This may not be acceptable to our partner. A couple's emotional balance will only be restored when confidence in one another is re-established.

THE ATTACHMENT PATTERNS OF ADULTS

The securely attached adult:

- is able to show and receive love;
- is able to give and receive comfort;
- can ask for help, if necessary;
- can form an attachment without losing him or herself;
- has a sense of security in him- or herself;
- is able to both feel and act in response to other people.

The insecurely attached adult (insecure/anxious behaviour):

- may be perceived as clinging;
- may be excessively attentive to other people's reactions;
- may have problems with separation;
- may have a need for continuous contact;

- may give up his or her own identity in exchange for attachment;
- may idealize partners and overlook faults in order to avoid separation;
- is able to feel but has difficulty in taking action in response to others.

The insecurely attached adult (insecure/dismissive behaviour):

- may form attachments to objects, work, projects;
- may have a tendency to compulsive self-sufficiency;
- may feel discomfort in social situations;
- may have a tendency to reject help and want to work alone;
- may have a tendency to withdraw and intellectualize;
- may have difficulties relating to major events in life that involve attachment;
- is capable of taking action, but has difficulty sharing feelings with others.

FROM OLD PATTERNS TO NEW OPPORTUNITIES

Our attachment behaviour and survival strategies will also be activated as adults when we encounter situations in our lives that remind us of feelings of need, betrayal, and insecurity which we know from childhood, deep down in our souls. Our attachment pattern functioned very well as our survival strategy when we were children and it was needed in order to get by. The attachment pattern gave us nurture and closeness in the best possible ways, while also protecting us against insecurity.

The survival strategies have become a major part of who we are – habits we use to protect ourselves. However, for many of us, they come at a very high price. Hence, we may benefit immensely by understanding how our old survival strategies prevent us from getting the connection and intimacy we long for as adults. The survival strategies may also prevent us from expressing important aspects of ourselves.

These aspects of our personality include emotions such as showing vulnerability, expressing anxiety and anger, or enjoying ourselves and devoting ourselves to each other. If we do not take charge of these survival strategies and bring them into the light so that we do not need to continue hiding aspects of our personality, the survival strategies will increase the distance between us. We might still be able to find energy for our children and our work and to continue our couple relationship, but an ever-increasing distance will separate us and cause conflict, frustration, or aggression.

When we, as adults, form couples and experience that we are really being heard and understood, then we relax, feel safe and secure, and we begin to develop an understanding of ourselves. When we feel like that, we do not have problems sharing our doubts, insecurity, and challenges with each other. In these situations, our emotions shuttle between us and we are able to investigate and unfold our "stories" together. In this way, we develop the acknowledging intimacy based on predictable attentiveness, which allows us to attempt to try out new ways of acting together.

THE PATTERNS ARE WORKABLE ALSO IN ADULTS

Attachment is a universal theme which continually shapes and influences our lives. It can give so much new hope and optimism when we become able to share with our partners what lies behind our survival strategies (the emotions which our attachment behaviour protects us from), then we immediately feel the intimacy with our partner. Suddenly, our relationship becomes warmer, closer, and more confident. Our original pattern of attachment, which we bring with us into the relationship and into parenthood, can be developed throughout our life for the benefit of not just ourselves, but also our partner, our relationship, and parenthood, and, thereby, also our children. If we were not so privileged as to develop a secure attachment in our childhood, it is possible to acquire secure attachment. Even when it can be hard work to give up destructive survival strategies, we are confident that when you turn the dream of your relationship, as well as your family, into reality, this is one of the pathways for your development.

24

THE LOGBOOK
OF THE SHIP
"HENRY DAVID) THOREAU"

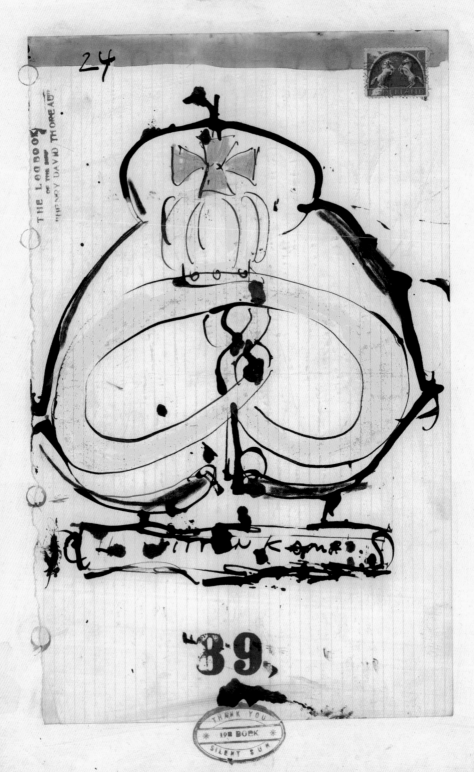

39

THANK YOU
198 BOOK
SILENT SUM

REFLECTIONS

Reading about attachment patterns, you might begin to reflect on your own attachment patterns. *Use* your experience when reflecting on the following questions as an opportunity to understand some of the frustrations in your daily life. One day, when you and your partner have plenty of time, you can tell him or her about your preoccupations. You may write down your thoughts in a journal. Hurtful memories tend to disappear very quickly in this way.

1. How did it feel when you needed your parents' help or comfort? What did they do and what did you do yourself when you were separated from them? Did you feel insecure and were you in some way affected emotionally?

2. What do you do when, in your daily life with your partner, you feel sad, angry, or rejected? What are your most vulnerable parts? What are your preferred responses – your survival strategies?
   - do you relate your thoughts and feelings in a calm and quiet way?
   - do you withdraw?
   - do you attack your partner, criticize or scold him or her?

3. In which ways do you respond now as an adult to your own child when you are under pressure, stressed, or in other ways feel insecure?

4. How do you share your reflections on this issue with your partner? How does your partner respond to your way of being with your child?

5. How do you feel about talking to your friends about your children? What do you and your partner say to each other about your parenting?

6. What effect do you think your childhood has had on your adult life overall , including the ways in which you see yourself and the ways you relate to your children?

AMERICAN IRONS

THE
TRUTH

ALWAYS
HAPPENS

AFGEGEVEN 1 AUG. 1970

× ZeSdE BoEk ×
THE KING OF
SUMMER

THE BRAIN –
OUR INVISIBLE GREENHOUSE

Acknowledging intimacy is a crucial factor in brain development. Science now informs us that the countless small, affirming episodes of acknowledging intimacy, which the child ideally experiences, release cascades of growth substances that stimulate neural networks in children's brains. The effect can be traced right down to cell level, where these substances interact with the genes, constructing and expanding the various sectors of the brain and the connections between them.

According to the latest brain research, this means that when we fill our family life with curiosity, openness, attention, imagination, warmth, love, and continual support, then we provide our children with optimal conditions for the healthy development of their brains.

For this reason, it is advantageous to pay attention to brain development, as it is an important element in the formation of our children's personality and an important way to understand why we and our children behave the way we do. The formation of identity and personality is just as much an expression of brain development that evolves through our parental influence.

Previously, it was believed that a human being's strong and weak qualities, abilities, and uniqueness were determined at birth and were, to a great extent, hereditary. However, recent research tells us that this is far from correct! Our personality is formed as the brain develops, and unfortunately, the brain only develops healthily given the right circumstances. Your child's development is, in other words, determined by a sustained and effective contact and attachment to you and a close circle of significant others.

The brain we are born with is not a fully developed entity. The brain is an organ which we can and must continue to develop and expand, since the brain stops developing only when dementia or death sets in. So, there are plenty of reasons for old and young alike to keep on challenging the brain.

ACKNOWLEDGING INTIMACY AS A PREREQUISITE FOR "FINE WIRING"

It all begins with the mind-blowing fact that your newborn infant lying quietly in front of you is actually born in the middle of a continuous growth spurt. This is not obvious if you are not aware of it!

Brain development is not a steady, continuous process. It happens at a very varied pace. Your child's first brain spurt begins in the right hemisphere a month before birth and continues until the age of two, approximately. During this period, all the major structures in the brain are formed and they will be with us for the rest of our lives.

As a parent, you need to participate in the growth spurt from day one. In the beginning, you have to regulate your speed to a calm, observing, acknowledging, attentive, supportive, full-contact presence, with all senses open. Newborn infants need and invite this type of contact. With this knowledge, it becomes even more meaningful to be just the way nature encourages us to be as young parents. We also feel that it makes sense to continue this process – even when we do not have time, or perhaps no longer feel like it.

The brain is divided into a left and a right hemisphere. Until your child starts school, the brain's primary development consists in establishing connecting pathways between the two hemispheres and other areas of the brain – like a kind of phone wiring. This helps the children gradually begin to use the brain's infinite number of options. As the numerous connections between the brain's many sections are established, the child develops the ability to co-ordinate messages and experiences from various sections of the brain. During these first years of our children's lives, our intimacy or lack of attention has a decisive influence on the pathways established or not and the quality of these connections.

EXPRESSING EMOTIONS AND THOUGHTS

Being able to feel and describe his or her own and other people's emotions and thoughts is the child's next step towards developing an ability for acknowledging intimacy. Until the "phone wiring" between the hemispheres has been developed, by the age of five or six, children do not have many words to describe the emotions they experience. They are not sure when it comes to using words to describe their feelings. At this developmental stage, your child is not yet able to separate him or herself from a feeling and use words to describe a feeling. In this situation, the most reassuring thing you can do is to not demand that your child should tell you what he or she feels. Instead, you may offer some suggestions as to the possible emotions you think could be in play.

I KNOW THE FEELING

Mother picks up Sophie in the kindergarten. Sophie stands next to Catherine and they talk about playing together. Catherine's mother says that unfortunately Catherine is unable to play, since they are visiting grandmother. In the car on the way home, Sophie is quiet and moody. Mother says, "I understand that you are sad and disappointed. You always play so well with Catherine and now you do not have anyone to play with. Is that how you feel?" Sophie cries a little, nods, and begins to talk about some of the things she has experienced in kindergarten today . . .

The whole of our nervous system is constructed in such a way that a child at a very early age experiences other people's thoughts and emotions. As parents, we more or less initiate our children's brain development by the way we interact with them. From birth to young adulthood, children develop many different abilities and qualities. However, during the entire process, children need the same type of input from we parents. They need us to be available to interact with them. This means that, through acknowledging intimacy, we constantly re-establish the balance whenever we experience a disconnection.

Conversely, inadequate emotional support without acknowledging intimacy in childhood unfortunately means that our child develops a reduced or fragile ability to experience connection. This means that the child embraces life with less energy, faulty judgement, and a general lack of control of his or her emotions and reactions.

Stress in a child can also result in the inhibition of healthy brain development. Particularly, stress of an unpredictable, frequent, or continuous nature can be harmful to the development of the brain. Stress occurs in children when we parents are not attuned to our child, when we cannot sense his or her unrest, when we cannot restore the balance of emotions, the closeness and the contact which our child needs more than anything when he or she is under pressure.

The good news for stressed parents of teenagers is that the development of the brain and the capacity for acknowledging intimacy extends into the teenage years. In fact, the brain only enters its decisive phase of development and functioning after the fifteenth year. The result is a positive development of a great number of functions and abilities, such as the ability to learn from emotions and use insight to form experiences, the ability to think strategically and regulate emotions. So, even if the youngsters may look fully developed at age fifteen, their brains are not.

As parents, we are acting as the sculptors of our child's brain. The brain is shaped by strong emotional experiences, on the basis of which its structure is formed. This structure will determine your child's emotional and intellectual development, as well as the way he or she behaves in life. Hence, it seems necessary for parents to discover and use those behaviours that provide the best options for promoting healthy brain development. We should also take care to hinder influences that inhibit healthy brain development. However, the challenges do not stop here. The human connections and close relationships we form later in life continue to have a major influence on the ways in which our brains are shaped and formed, so it is important to nurture, develop, and expand the acknowledging intimacy throughout our lives.

WHAT INQUIRING MINDS NEED TO KNOW ABOUT THE BRAIN

The human brain is the most complex biological structure on the planet. All the major differences that separate us from our closest relative, the chimpanzee, and everything else in the animal kingdom, are contained in our brain. It has been said about the brain that it is not a computer, it is a jungle. This expression could well cover the enormous and immensely complex contents, which only recently have been mapped by science. The brain is also the human organ which is least developed at birth, even though all the major brain structures are already established in an immature form by the fifth month of the pregnancy.

The brain, which at birth weighs approximately 400 grams, will, in the course of the first year, grow almost to the adult weight of one kilo. The cerebral cortex is the structure which gains the major part of the additional weight, since only one third of the cerebral cortex is present at birth. The rest is developed during the first two to three years, and it will take the next 14–18 years to reach maturity. This is where we parents play a central part in the comprehensive shaping of the brain.

THE EMOTIONS IN THE BRAIN

"The emotional brain", where all our feelings, sensations, and experiences are co-ordinated and stored, is developed from birth in the right frontal lobe. This is where the development of compassion and empathy takes place. This means that the right frontal lobe, from the very beginning, is involved in such central human functions as social adaptation, control of mood, ambition, and responsibility. Both frontal lobes in the cerebral cortex are also the only structure in the brain that has a direct connection to the centres that respond to danger with fight, flight, or freeze reactions, which are located at deep levels in the brain. Hence, the frontal lobes are also called "the brain's manager". This means that if we want to change reactive patterns of behaviour, or put a damper on stress in the body, then it will be "the manager" that makes it happen. The right frontal lobe, which is engaged in processing emotions, begins to mature in the ninth month, and continues to develop at full speed until the second year of the child's life.

The frontal lobe in the left hemisphere is activated a little later, in the middle of the second year. Here, language functions and related functions of consciousness are lodged.

Previous research established that the difference between the functions of the frontal lobes was so great that the left frontal lobe merited the name "the intellectual brain" and the right frontal lobe "the emotional brain". However, recent research demonstrates that only the language function and the functions associated with language are located in the left frontal lobe, while all other functions of the adult brain seem to be more evenly distributed in both frontal lobes (Morten Kringelbach, 2004).

OUR BRAINS' BUILT-IN AUTOPILOTS

In the following, we shall describe two automatic reactions of the brain which can cause children, couples, and parents great difficulties. However, they are not so automatic that we parents cannot have a major influence on how these processes develop and unfold in ourselves and in our children. We have chosen to call the two automatic reactions "the cogwheels" and "the shame trap".

CYCLING METAPHORS

The large and the small cogwheels are concepts from the world of cycling. The cogwheels are the toothed wheels that are applied when the terrain changes. Hence, you change gears from the small cogwheel used in hilly and trackless terrain to the large cogwheel's pleasant pace in flat country.

We are all familiar with cycling on the large and the small cogwheels. Some of us tend to spend time using one of the cogwheels more than the other, while others find it easier to change gears more often. Like the bicycle, our brain cannot function using both cogwheels simultaneously. Using this metaphor, it is always the "small cogwheel" in the brain that is activated when we feel endangered or exposed, or simply experience something that seems to be unsafe.

We begin by describing "the cogwheels", which consist of two very different ways of processing experiences. The small cogwheel works fast and is impulsive. The large cogwheel works more slowly and is a more reflective and slower process. Human beings have the capacity to move between these brain functions – that is what we call "changing gears".

THE SMALL COGWHEEL

At its simplest, the function of the small cogwheel is to ensure our survival in situations where we may experience that our life is in danger. When our nervous system functions on the small cogwheel, we are at the mercy of our basic instincts and accumulated experiences. We are prone to fight, flee, or freeze, and our responses are uninhibited, impulsive. All these reactions can be efficient when we need to survive. The problem is that in our daily lives, we are rarely confronted by a hungry tiger. If we are reminded of forceful events from our childhood, our brain does not distinguish between those events and external stimuli, and reacts to everything that is perceived as unsafe or dangerous using the small cogwheel.

This is the reason why we adults can immediately react to loud discussions as if they were dangerous. A reason for this could be that when we were children, we were scared stiff by the alarming atmosphere created when our parents fought and mother began to cry. On a deeper level, the older part of the brain, which stores repeated experiences of this kind, is still very much alive and ready to be activated – the small cogwheel.

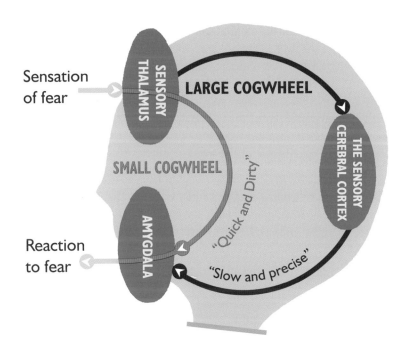

Sensation of fear

LARGE COGWHEEL

SENSORY THALAMUS

THE SENSORY CEREBRAL CORTEX

SMALL COGWHEEL

"Quick and Dirty"

AMYGDALA

Reaction to fear

"Slow and precise"

A section of the brain with a schematic indication of the pathways of fear. The anatomical position and proportion in relation to the silhouette are not correct, but we have chosen to use it in order to simplify the following figures. The sensory signal reaches the sensory thalamus. When the signal is interpreted as an expression of something "dangerous", the impulse quickly changes to the small cogwheel-"quick and dirty" – to the amygdala, the minute centre which controls the fight, flight, and freeze reaction of fear. If the signal is interpreted as "not dangerous", it continues on to the large cogwheel, which is slow and precise, and moves the process into the sensory cerebral cortex, where it is processed by all the relevant higher functions (experience, logic, language, imagination, etc.) which contribute to the creation of meaning, followed by a matched, nuanced, and relevant action. The process could be described as a "circuit breaker" in the sensory thalamus, an either/or enabling a change of gears between the two cogwheels!

(Inspired by J. LeDoux: *The Synaptic Self,* Penguin 2002)

Our patterns of reacting to fear and threats, which we develop as children, we carry into our adult lives, where the reality is that there is not much that is so dangerous that it is necessary to activate the survival strategies. However, the deeper layers of the brain, which activate the survival strategies, do not grow more discerning or wiser as we get older, and they continue to function according to gut feelings. The result is that when something on a sensory level resembles an event that was once life threatening, in the deep parts of the brain survival strategies are immediately launched. This process will continue until we become aware of how we can counter the automatic impulse and find alternative responses.

When we, as adults, experience something that reminds us of danger, we automatically change gears to the small cogwheel. We tend to do this before we think twice and before we discover that there was no reason to be afraid.

Being on the small cogwheel is, therefore, an indication that we are driven by a survival strategy as, for some reason or other, we feel under pressure, sad, rejected, insecure, angry, or threatened. Some of us might, for instance, have difficulties accepting criticism – perhaps because we were constantly subjected to criticism as children. In this case, our brain perceives the scenario as threatening and unpleasant, we lose our bearings, and go straight to the small cogwheel as soon as we experience criticism. Functioning on the small cogwheel makes us say and do things that normally we would not say or do. We tend then to pull the trigger before we think, our temper reaches boiling point, or we withdraw into ourselves, or freeze completely. (The fight–flight–freeze reactions.)

In children, we see the small cogwheel in action when, for instance, they go berserk in hot snowsuits in Tesco, or appear to go out of their mind, crying and fuming when an older sibling keeps on teasing. In adults, the dogfights, the power struggles, and the hurtful confrontations abound when we are welded to the small cogwheel. This is when we adults begin to throw things at each other verbally and, occasionally, physically, or say unforgivable things to our children. When we are on the small cogwheel, we are beside ourselves and we are, quite frankly, out of control.

THE SMALL COGWHEEL "THE DOGFIGHT"

A couple in the middle of a fight on the small cogwheel:
No development at all

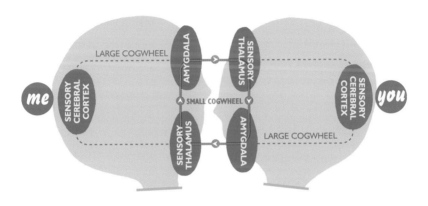

THE SMALL COGWHEEL "SCOLDING!"

Parent and child on the small cogwheel: "Scolding".
No development. Who is the eldest?

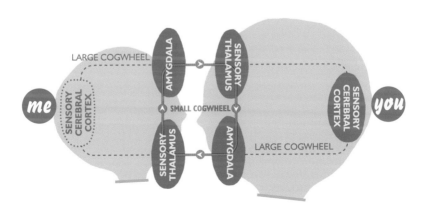

Functioning in the small cogwheel is a completely natural response for young children. Their reactions are entirely spontaneous and, at times, extremely noisy. The good news is that we should be pleased about this. If, from the outset, the child was geared to ask for food politely and calmly, well, the child mortality rate would probably look different! To start with, this capacity has ensured our own, and later our children's, survival. As parents, it is our most important task to respond appropriately to this demand.

If we look at our children when they are on the small cogwheel, we find that it is the child's own sensitivity to experiences of insecurity, stress, unrest, physical discomfort, tiredness, or shock which is decisive, and not what we adults may think. This can be completely irrelevant, and then we do not comfort our child by saying:

You should not be sad about that . . .

There . . . You should stop crying now . . .

Well, it was not as bad as all that . . .

What the child needs most at this point is an adult who stays on the large cogwheel. This means an adult who is able to maintain an acknowledging intimacy with the child.

So, instead, we might say:

You are sad and it hurts so much. Come here and let me give you a cuddle.

I understand that you want to stay out longer. There are others who are allowed to stay out for much longer, and you could quickly begin to feel isolated. However, I feel less uneasy when you arrive home at the time we agreed.

I told you that you were not allowed to do this. And you were sad – I understand your sadness really well.

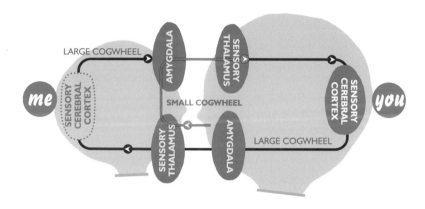

Parent and child beginning a dialogue in order to restore the relationship. The adult has changed to the large cogwheel and is able to give the child what he or she needs most: development of the large cogwheel!

Acknowledging intimacy is not a miracle cure designed to airbrush the small cogwheel away. We neither can nor should remove the small cogwheel, because it represents the energy that triggers emotions and it helps us learn more about each other. The objective is not to get our children to be in a better mood, but to acknowledge the emotions children experience when they are on the small cogwheel. In this way, they will experience the feeling to the full and learn to return to the large cogwheel in their own time. The conflict about the differences should not be solved, but the confrontation should be dissolved.

Hence, the challenge is to take an interest in how we can be present on the large cogwheel instead of focusing on how to get children to stop being on the small cogwheel.

THE QUIET PACE OF THE LARGE COGWHEEL

The large cogwheel represents the brain's alternative pattern of response, when there is no danger. Here, the brain co-ordinates experience, nuanced memories, language skills, humour, logic, and all the other advanced functions of the brain that we are not necessarily able to access when we are in the middle of a crisis. However, it is when we are on the large cogwheel that we are capable of containing other people, listening and not just jumping to quick conclusions. The availability of all the other large cogwheel capacities that constitute the person is determined by being on the large cogwheel, which allows us to develop our ability to stay focused and be close to other people. It is on the large cogwheel that we can develop all our good and appropriate mastery skills.

"THE LARGE COGWHEEL"

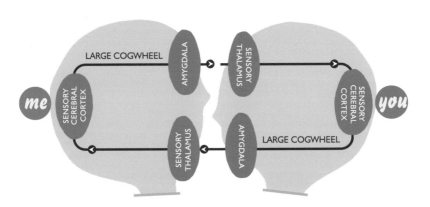

A couple in an ordinary conversation in the large cogwheel: development

For instance:

- finding our emotional balance, whether it concerns anxiety, stress, anger, etc.;

- developing empathy towards the people with whom we are in touch;

- being able to take appropriate action to the needs of ourselves and others;

- developing a considerate way of being together with other people;

- getting insight about ourselves and others.

Primordial man needed a survival strategy, which is why the small cogwheel is so quickly activated. So, that is why our experience is that we can quickly blow our top before we have thought something through. In terms of solving problems in our relationship with our partner and children, those milliseconds are terribly important. With its well-considered, cogent way of solving problems, the large cogwheel is slower to take action and does not automatically override the activity of the small cogwheel. We have to work on that.

CHANGING GEARS

Here, we are talking about an either/or situation between the large and the small cogwheel and, thus, a possible shift between the cogwheels. We have the opportunity to learn how to move between the cogwheels – what we call "changing gears". Changing gears is a considerable challenge to many of us in our close relationships. A divorce rate of 40% might be a conservative estimate of the fact that, in close relationships, there are very many emotions capable of activating our small cogwheels and keeping us in a vicious circle.

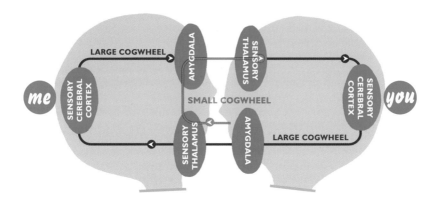

A couple in the Acknowledging Dialogue where one has changed gears from the small to the large cogwheel: Emerging development

However, instead of the doomsday scenario, we could begin to look at the opportunities to use our personal cogwheels in a more synchronized way together. We could begin by taking an interest in the extremely important change of gears and how this will enable us to make a swift return to the acknowledging intimacy experienced only when we are on the large cogwheel. The major challenge is that the extent to which we learn to use the small or the large cogwheel is quite individual. The decisive factor is the degree to which we, as children, received help to master our difficult emotions and the extent to which our efforts were acknowledged. We might have a history characterized by more or less "luck" in the process of changing gears from the small to the large cogwheel. So, we should not only help our children learn to cycle, we should also support them when they are using the large cogwheel. We should teach them how to change gears, so they can get off the small cogwheel when it tries to take over.

MOTHER ON THE LARGE COGWHEEL

Mother and Christian, aged five, are expecting visitors, but they are running a little late. While mother is cooking, she encourages Christian to clear away his Lego. However, Christian plays on – he does not want to stop, and instead he begins to throw the Lego blocks around. "Come on," his mother says, with the result that Christian becomes very angry and pours the entire box of Lego out on to the floor.

At this point, mother has a choice: getting angry and scolding Christian, using the small cogwheel and risking going out of control so that both she and Christian will be beside themselves when the guests arrive. Alternatively, she could stay on the large cogwheel and help Christian out of this situation.

She chooses the second option. She sits down on the floor next to him and begins to help him voice his feelings: "You were just playing so well, what a pity you have to stop. I can see that clearing all this away is a huge job."

The mother re-establishes contact so that Christian feels she senses his state of mind. Then he gradually begins to change gears from the small to the large cogwheel.

"Come along Christian, now we'll sit down and clean all this up so we can really look forward to Granny coming over for dinner. Do you know what we are having?"

They enter into a flow. Both feel on top of the situation again and are ready to receive Granny.

When we inadvertently find ourselves on the small cogwheel, we start what we could call a temporary brain short-circuit. All the advanced mental functions normally at our disposal are beyond our reach. We are completely unaware of the possibility of changing gears to get on to the large cogwheel! However, we can help each other change gears to the large cogwheel. Here and now it seems almost impossible to move on to the large cogwheel, when I am mega angry, mega hysterical, or hurt. You can, however, be quite confident that moving on to the large cogwheel will be a whole lot easier when you practise with others! Changing gears becomes easier the more you and your child practise this, because the brain learns to respond automatically in a new way. You will notice immediately how the surrounding world welcomes this change in you with open arms. Only when we decide to acknowledge and listen instead of letting it all hang out when we have lost control can we restore the situation in ways that not only our children, but also our relationship, so desperately need. It doesn't just feel good, safe, and right when we do it – it feels almost blissful to be able to accomplish such a change of gears from the small to the large cogwheel.

The best part is that our children automatically learn this way to change gears if we, as a couple and as mother or father, respectively, become role models. As we develop our ability to stay on the large cogwheel – being attentive, sensing and guiding our impulses, listening and reflecting – or our ability to change gears from the small to the large cogwheel, then it automatically rubs off on our children. The beauty of it is that we can, as it were, oil our cogwheels. By practising together and being conscious of where we are, the result is that we continue to improve our ability to change gears from the small to the large cogwheel. After conflicts or distancing, we all need restoration to happen quickly. Hence, it is important, if we have not already learnt it, that we learn to master how to change gears quickly.

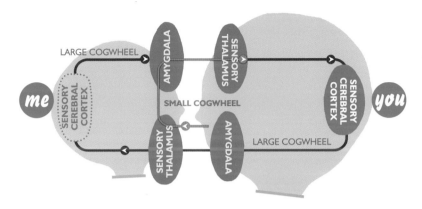

Parent and child in an Acknowledging Dialogue with restoration of the contact. The adult has moved on to the large cogwheel and is then able to begin giving what the child needs most: development of his or her large cogwheel!

Whether or not the changing of gears actually takes place in a flowing, natural way depends on our capacity for commitment and risk taking. However, unfortunately, this is not always enough. The success of the mission depends on whether or not our child or our partner experiences a new, positive calm and balance. This is the core issue! Even when we think that we are being attentive as well as empathetic, it is our child's experience of the atmosphere at home that makes it possible for him or her to move from the small cogwheel to the large that counts!

Parent mood swings from positive to negative emotional states and vice versa are stressful experiences for children and, therefore, the greatest challenge of parenting. It is quite certain that this is the point where the differences between us as parents can become most evident, surprising and unwanted as they often are. Whether we like it or not, this is where our different rhythms, sensitivities, and opinions about the way we raise our children are expressed: *That is how it is! That is the way I like it. You are just so stupid!* This is where neither parent gets their way and nobody will give in. Only when we parents try out a different approach can we find out what would be a better approach.

1. YOUR OWN COGWHEELS

How do you respond when you are on the small cogwheel?

What does it feel like for you to be on the small cogwheel?

Which emotions and situations drive you on to the small cogwheel?

Do you know what it feels like to move from the small to the large cogwheel (the shifting gears) or the other way round?

2. ON THE COGWHEELS WITH YOUR PARTNER

What does your partner do that makes it easy or difficult for you to move from the small to the large cogwheel?

What does your partner do when you are on the small cogwheel?

3. ON THE COGWHEELS WITH YOUR CHILD

When do you and your child find yourselves move on to the small cogwheel?

How do you, as a parent, respond to your child when you are on the large cogwheel?

How do you feel when you are on the large cogwheel?

What would make it easier for you to change gear between the cogwheels?

4. ON THE COGWHEELS WITH THE FAMILY

What does my partner do when I am on the small cogwheel with our child?

What do I do when my partner is on the small cogwheel with our child?

One day, when you and your partner have plenty of time, you could tell him or her about the thoughts that came to you when you began to reflect on your own cogwheels. It might be a good idea to write down these thoughts.

THE SHAME TRAP – POISON FOR THE BRAIN

The shame trap is yet another automatic reaction found in our nervous system. It signifies a collision between two different sections of the nervous system and occurs when we are preoccupied with one activity and then someone suddenly bawls us out, rejects us, or something similar. When these two sections are affected at the same time, we respond in the same way as when you use the accelerator and the brake at the same time. Both the car and the brain screech to a grinding halt! Both car and the human brain are built for using either accelerator or brake, so the result is a short-circuit. It is as if the helium has fizzled out of the balloon: we blush; we feel as if we lose face and might even lose our voice. Seen from the outside, it looks as if the child is collapsing. A trap was set and now someone is caught!

JENS IN THE SHAME TRAP

Jens is seven years old. He returns home after an important football match. He is proud and happy because, for the first time, he has scored three of the five goals which secured a victory for his team. Father is taking a nap on the couch after a long day at work. He does not look at Jens, hears some of the words, and turns away, saying, "Please do not make such a din . . . can't you see that I am having a rest!" Jens runs into his room.

Jens is trapped. He was full of curiosity, joy, expectation, and energy, but he was suddenly interrupted by a father who turns away and, in a grumpy and angry voice, makes a bombastic demand: "You are not allowed to do what you are doing . . . stop it at once . . . how many times have I told you . . ."

Jens looks as if he has been struck by lightning. His arms are dangling, his head is sinking, and tears are about to roll down his cheeks. A trap has slammed shut! And it is extremely unpleasant for him.

The combination of the accelerator and the brake occurs when we are concentrating on doing something that excites us and makes us happy and suddenly we are confronted by an unexpected wall of resistance, full of *Ugh, you ought to be ashamed of yourself, you should not do that, I am deeply disappointed* or *I do not have the time and I do not feel like listening to or watching what you do . . .*

Such clashes often happen to us over small and large issues. The reason we are drawing attention to the problem here is to highlight the importance of helping our children out of the shame trap. We do not realize how important this restoration of balance is. Often, we do not understand that we leave our child in a helpless situation where he or she feels abandoned and sad. Our child feels left alone and is challenged with the task of finding a way out of the emotional chaos of the shame trap.

So, when we ground our child to give him or her time to calm down and consider why he or she freaked out completely during dinner, then we must understand that the child is incapable of this kind of reflection at that time. The child has been caught in the shame trap – accelerator and brake were applied simultaneously – and now he or she does not have the ability to think rationally or recreate the calm. Our child's brain has quite simply not reached a stage in its development where this is possible. The only way our child is able to move on and leave the emotional chaos behind is through interaction with another human being.

At first glance, it may seem as if the child is cooling off and calming down, but, in actual fact, he or she often resorts to survival strategies in order to be able to tolerate being alone and grounded. Perhaps the child becomes even more furious (fight), perhaps he or she escapes into some activity or distracting thoughts (flight), or perhaps he or she gives up as a way of complying in the situation (freeze).

If children experience getting caught in the shame trap without being helped out again, there is a heavy price to pay. The price is the breach of confidence in us as adults, because the children

Above: "The shame trap" has slammed shut, the child has lost energy, is paralysed, shamed, and experiences itself as alone in the world.

Below: "The shame trap" is opened by the only person who is able to do so. The adult takes the initiative to restore the connection.

dare not believe again that we would help them when they are in trouble. To a child, it seems that we parents reinforce their need for survival strategies.

It is not a single experience of the shame trap, but a recurring pattern of these experiences that turn out to have a direct, growth-inhibiting effect on children. To adults, the shame trap is also extremely disturbing, because it paralyses us, disturbs our energy, and closes us down. The risk of growth-inhibiting shame is greatest in the child's first years. We may have resorted to shaming as part of our child-rearing, and later in life use it as a means of control without considering or even noticing the consequences.

It is important to stress that the goal is not to avoid conflict in relationships, not to avoid having limits, and not to refrain from expressing one's honest opinion in order to avoid the shame trap. It is, however, important that we realize how vital our use of acknowledging intimacy is in helping our children, and sometimes our partner, to escape from the shame trap.

When children find themselves in the shame trap, they need immediate restoration of contact and closeness. In terms of brain development, children are not sufficiently developed to do this for themselves. In addition, when in such a situation, they are not able to reach out for what they most need. A significant adult on the large cogwheel is needed to help the child find his or her way back to a place of safe and confident connection.

Since the development of the child's brain during this stage is occurring at the speed of light, it is important that restoration occurs in the here and now. Even momentary stressful conditions during the brain's growth spurts tend to shape the brain so that more permanent traits and characteristics are created and make the brain extra vulnerable to stress and strain later in life. Clearly, unfortunate development like this depends on the presence of a number of factors, and it is impossible to be definitive.

Repeated experience of restoration has the effect that, time and again, children experience that they can emerge on the other side of trauma with increased trust and security in their circle of significant others.

As parents, we should, therefore, be very mindful that we do things for our children that our children cannot do for themselves because of their developing brain. This process gives children a liberating and amazing feeling of relief that it is possible to change gear from the small to the large cogwheel and re-establish the acknowledging intimacy.

. . . AND OUT OF THE SHAME TRAP

Having tossed and turned, the father finds it difficult to continue his nap. Jens' energy disturbs him and he can hear that his son is walking around, making noises in his room. He gets up and goes to Jens' room. Jens is furious and dismissive. The father apologizes sincerely. It was wrong not to wake up and listen to Jens' wonderful story. The father says that he is sorry about the way it happened and continues, "I understand very well that you are proud of having scored three goals, and I am very happy that you come home and tell me about it, but I was not listening properly."

Jens begins to cry, but brightens up and slowly relates some incidents from the exciting match. Father listens. They continue talking about the match around the dinner table, where the two younger siblings want to hear about it again. Jens scored three goals!

THE SHAME TRAP FOR ADULTS

The difference between being a child and an adult is that we adults have learnt quite a number of ways to escape from the shame trap. However, the shame trap might still be activated at any given time among adults.

In some respects, the shame trap functions in the same way for adults as for children:

. . . You do your best; you are goal-orientated, full of energy, and perhaps in a good mood. You are not that aware of what is going on around you. Then it happens! Your partner says or does something which hurts you profoundly! Shock! The words disappear. Suddenly, you feel as if you were struck by lightning, you feel ashamed, and, if you are in the company of others, you feel that you "lose face", which only makes everything worse. You feel embarrassed and think *how could I?* The malaise is paralysing and there seems to be no way out! The trap has slammed shut . . .!

The shame trap is also difficult to handle for adults alone. Just like our children, we need a gentle, considerate opening into acknowledging intimacy in the company of the person whose behaviour triggered us into the shame trap. The truth is that your reaction is about yourself and not about your partner, who quite inadvertently happens to trigger your shame trap response. However, we do not feel that when caught in the trap. The reflecting part of our brain is on hold. At first, we do not feel anything but shame. We feel that we have lost our bearings and later we might feel anger towards the person who we feel shamed us.

Getting caught in the shame trap is an obvious chance to allow ourselves to learn new things about our personality structure. When we find ourselves in the shame trap and the big emotions are present, these emotions are always linked with old experiences of being shamed when we were children. As adults, we can begin to respond differently to shaming experiences, since we are no longer children and no longer alone. Now we are with someone, our partner, who, with his or her acknowledging intimacy, can help us out of our shame trap, contributing to our partner's, our children's, and our own further development.

REFLECTIONS

1. Describe the scenario when you last saw your child get caught in the shame trap.
    Describe the scenario when you last saw your partner get caught in the shame trap.
    Describe the scenario when you last got caught in the shame trap.

2. How did your child react when he or she was caught in the shame trap?
    How did your partner react when he or she was caught in the shame trap?
    How did you react when you were caught in the shame trap?

3. How did you feel when you were caught in the shame trap?

4. What might your child subsequently have needed in order to restore connection and confidence?
    What might your partner subsequently have needed in order to restore connection and confidence?
    What might you subsequently have needed in order to restore connection and confidence?

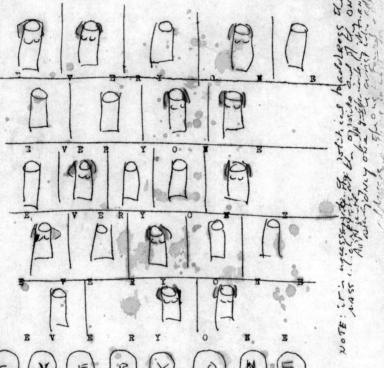

THE TRANSFORMATIVE POWER
OF STORYTELLING

The stories we tell or imagine about ourselves, our child, our partner, or family are always important. The reason for this is that whether we are young or old, our narratives of self contribute to the creation of understanding of ourselves. Our beliefs about the world and about ourselves are formed through stories. Stories help us to construct meaning in our lives and the events we witness. By increasing our understanding of self, and by exploring the events in our lives, our story about ourselves will develop and expand.

As we grow up, we are automatically constantly registering what goes on in ourselves and in others. This data constitutes the basis of the autobiographical story we all have in our baggage.

However, this multi-layered autobiography is not the definitive truth. It undergoes changes, and nuances occur as we explore it with our partner or significant others. When we do that, we add new layers to our autobiographical understanding, which makes it possible for us to change and to act differently.

When adults and children tell stories about themselves:

- they can create cohesion between our experience now and earlier experiences;
- they create new opportunities for ourselves instead of getting stuck and repeating old stories.

So, it is very valuable to help our children make meaning of what they think and experience, by inviting them to tell us what they have been doing, what is happening here and now, and what they would like to happen in their lives in the future.

Regarding conflicts and difficulties in relationships, we also have some great and often unexplored opportunities for discovery when we activate the story's transformative power.

By exploring the untold stories in our lives, we can find clarity about what we actually feel, think, wish, like, or dislike. We can find out more about what we long for and why we react the way we do. The goal is that, through the story, and motivated by curiosity and wonder, we, along with our partner, will gain greater understanding of the connection between our present feelings and similar emotions and images we recollect from our childhood and youth.

This is when I, as a listener, have a curious and wondering attitude about where the powerful story we call the attachment story begins. I create the best conditions for my child's, my partner's, or my own emerging story that are able to create cohesion and meaning in our lives.

Most conflicts arise because of differences. Through our stories of these differences, now and in the past, we move away from conflict into a new understanding of ourselves, our partner, and our children.

OUR SIGNIFICANT STORY

Anders tells Eva about himself. He says he is psychologically strong, that he is robust, and that nothing can topple him. He says that it is important to be able to take care of yourself. That is, in fact, what he has done since he was quite young.

It is important to him, and he is proud of the fact that he is independent and takes care of himself. The flipside is that he does not want to be with another human being who wants to care for him and wants to relieve him of some of the responsibility.

Anders says that as a child he learnt that crying was not a way to get nurture and attention. On the contrary, his parents told him that there was no reason to cry. Besides the fact that he did not receive any comfort when he was sad, he was also told that he was wrong to feel sad. Conversely, he discovered that when he did some brave things or performed tasks that were difficult for his young age, then he got his parents' attention and praise. He felt seen. Throughout his childhood and youth he got the message: "Do not cry. Show that you are a strong person who can perform – then we will notice you and appreciate you." The resulting message was: "You must perform and achieve before you can enjoy life."

Eva tells Anders that when she helps other people, her self-esteem blossoms. She sees it as one of her strengths that she dares to feel her own vulnerability. She also feels that way about other people who dare to show their vulnerability. However, when she meets people who do not show their vulnerable sides, she doesn't know what role to play and feels insecure. She asks herself "what should I do if I am not supposed to help the other person?"

Eva talks about her childhood experiences. She grew up in a family where showing consideration for other people was the greatest of all virtues. So, when she showed her parents that she was capable of setting aside her own needs and focusing instead on her mother's needs especially, then she got the attention and the praise she wanted. Then she felt loved and appreciated. When she was sad, there was no shortage of nurture and comfort. Hence, the story she tells about herself is: "Be a nice and caring girl – then you will receive love and attention. You should not be afraid of showing your own vulnerability, since when you do, you will receive comfort. But for heaven's sake do not be egotistical. Do not do anything, and do not even feel like doing anything, that could hurt others. If you do it anyway, then we will have to reject you."

Anders is keen on teaching their child Henrik to become a strong and independent boy and not a sissy. When Henrik cries, Anders is anxious to draw him out of this state. On the other hand, Eva would like to see Henrik develop as an open and sensitive boy, who can feel his own and other people's emotions.

When Anders attempts to get Henrik to stop crying, Eva's beliefs about what is best for the child are activated. She experiences Anders' intervention as a catastrophe.

After Anders and Eva have begun listening to each other's attachment stories they have become more aware of how limited are their own beliefs about what is the "right" thing to do in relation to their child. They have begun to see new possibilities, not only as parents, but also as partners.

Anders and Eva have become aware that their differences, which are expressed very clearly in relation to Henrik, also have been and still are a core issue in their relationship.

PLEASE CALM DOWN!

We can be quite certain that when we are affected emotionally (angry, sad, hurt, or disappointed), either by the way in which our partner behaves towards our child or when our partner comments on our own parenting style, then a larger story is always operating backstage.

WHY HAVE YOU BOUGHT THE WRONG JUICE?

Hans is a man who tries to be an attentive father and a warm and obliging husband to his wife Sara. He is, for instance, aware of the fact that it means a lot to Sara that the food they eat is as healthy as possible and that they predominantly buy organic food and drinks. Hence, he makes an effort to buy organic food, even if that is not one of his own priorities. One day, when Sara is putting the goods Hans has bought into the fridge, she suddenly comments on his shopping with the words: "But Hans, this juice is made from concentrate . . ."

Hans immediately gets furious, makes a commotion and leaves, banging the door. Sara watches him, speechless.

We can probably all understand that Hans finds Sara's comment annoying. However, what we do not immediately understand – just like Sara and Hans do not – is why he reacts *so* strongly. They are not aware of all the issues involved in Hans' own personal story. When it is unfolded, Hans and Sara are able to understand better his strong reaction.

When Hans begins to explore his drastic response, he discovers that it is connected to his father. He was a tough type of man who would say things like: "It is fine that you won a bronze medal. It is too bad that you did not get gold." Hans's father mostly focused on getting his own needs satisfied. Hans's mother had a difficult time, and for most of his childhood and youth Hans had to listen to his mother's many problems and sorrows. He saw his mother's love as conditional on his lending an ear to her complaints. To Hans, all this meant that he as a child made the decision NEVER TO BECOME LIKE HIS FATHER. This decision means that Hans as a young man and as an adult decides his own value in a relationship on the basis of whether or not people are pleased when he does something for them.

So, when Sara is pleased with his shopping, everything is as it should be. But when Sara expresses dissatisfaction, she unsettles the foundation of his beliefs about himself and triggers an earthquake. Hans gets furious and walks away.

Maybe you wonder why Hans is prompted to think of his egotistical father because he bought the "wrong" juice? A precondition for being able to see such a connection is that we are convinced that such connections exist between our experiences here and now and our previous life events and childhood experiences. In addition, our partner should also be aware of this and be interested in exploring the story of this connection. This means that Hans's opportunity to talk about his childhood memories, elicited by a concrete situation here and now, depends on Sara's willingness to LISTEN to his story and her interest in doing so.

Even when these conditions exist, it is not necessarily easy to arrive at getting in touch with the specific childhood memories which are activated by the present situation. This capacity varies greatly from person to person. Some people have no difficulty; they immediately register which emotions are present and they quickly draw on childhood memories where some of the same emotions were prevalent. In such cases, many adults are able to tell vivid stories from their childhood.

Other adults encounter great difficulties in this process. They may have no immediate memories of anything, and a typical statement would be that they do not remember anything in particular. They had an excellent childhood and there is nothing more to say about that. But do not be discouraged – this is quite common. Fortunately, we all had a childhood, and we can all tease out these memories in time. Here are some sentences constructed to put you on the right track when you say them aloud to your partner.

Sentences that have the subtle effect of causing you to think about something could, for instance, be:

- That reminds me of . . .
- What I felt was that . . . and, as a result, the decision I took as a child was that . . .
- What I had to do in order to get by was . . .
- The way I chose to . . . was that . . .
- The way I was sure to get my mother's and father's affection was to . . .
- What I really longed for was to . . .
- The way it should have been was that . . .

It is important not to censor yourself and expect that what you say should be formulated in a clear and concise way. The most important thing is actually to create a space where words can emerge. Then more words will automatically be forthcoming.

A good metaphor for how our autobiographical stories can emerge is the stacks of trays found in some canteens. When you take out one tray the next emerges automatically, ready for use.

The same applies to the first sentences which are your "first tray". When one thing has been voiced and "the tray has been removed", the next sentence in your attachment story arrives automatically.

So, instead of saying *Please calm down! There is no reason to respond so disproportionately*, it would be advantageous if Sara instead later said, *Hans, I do not understand your severe reaction at all, but I would like to. Please try to tell me what it reminds you of.*

THE COLOURFUL AND COHERENT STORY IS THE BEST

When we tell and uncover new aspects of our own story in a situation of acknowledging intimacy with our partner, there will gradually be more coherence in our story and more colours and nuanced feelings will characterize the people involved.

The story may be colourful when it contains many descriptions of the emotions of the storyteller and the other characters involved. The story can be described as having coherence when the memories are interconnected over time to create a meaningful whole. In this way, the story will have more transformative significance to both parties – both in relation to the past and to the present challenges and opportunities.

In a way, the story can be understood both as a new narrative about the past and also as an expression of a new development in the direction of a greater overview and maturity in the person who tells the story. For this reason, the point is not to find the "right" story, or having told the "wrong" or untruthful story until now. The aim is to gradually develop an ability to create many nuanced stories about oneself. The more stories or images I can tell about myself, to myself and, therefore, also to others, the better it will be for me and the people I live with, because, in this way, it becomes easier to let go of the old patterns and make space for new opportunities together.

THE ATTACHMENT PATTERN AND THE STORIES ARE INTERCONNECTED

With this knowledge about the significance of our narratives, we can enable our children to get an early start in the creation of colourful, coherent stories about their lives. It turns out that there is a clear connection between the frequency of nuances in our story, its degree of coherence, and our attachment pattern. Adults with confident and secure attachment patterns are typically able to tell colourful, nuanced, and thoughtful autobiographical stories with a high degree of coherence.

An example could be: "I grew up in a family where we were very close. My parents were very loving and caring. My mother was always very ill and from an early age I learnt to attend to her needs – thereby also putting my own needs on hold. At first I was very worried and overprotective towards my own daughter. Again, I felt that the attention to my child and her needs filled my entire life. I did not feel that I could allow myself to fully experience my own needs if they were not related to my daughter's well-being – otherwise I would feel that I let her down. My boyfriend was naturally very unhappy about this."

It follows that adults with an insecure dismissive attachment pattern typically tell stories that are somewhat pale and thin, but coherent. Adults with an insecure anxious attachment pattern typically tell stories about themselves that are colourful, but incoherent.

In summary, we believe that, in addition to events from our childhood contributing to our mental health as adults, our present understanding of what happened to us as children also influences the way we live today. This demonstrates that through the continuing attachment narrative, we have the option of making changes in our adult lives by developing greater coherence in our narrative and a richer more colourful palette.

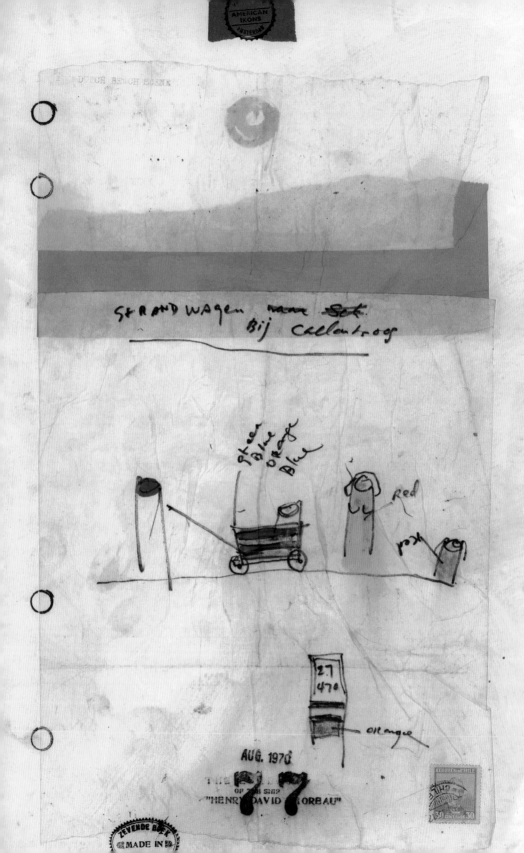

REFLECTIONS

If you are curious to know more about your own attachment pattern, then try to find answers to the following questions.

1. A SECURE BASE

As a child:

Who did you turn to when you were sad, ill, or tired?

Who do you think understood you best as a child?

Describe a couple of situations with your parents.

What was the most frightening situation or the most scary moment you experienced as a child?

How were you comforted as a child? Who comforted you?

Today:

What do you do when you are ill, worried, or tired?

Who do you turn to when you are agitated or worried?

In whose company do you feel most relaxed and at ease?

Do you ever feel cut off or excluded by anyone?

Are you ever afraid that the people you are close to will leave you? Do you cling to them even when that annoys them?

Is there a recurring pattern in your close relationships where you mediate, where you are the person who opens up, the strong person, the person in charge, the person who takes care of everybody else, the strong, silent provider?

In your close relationships, do you have a tendency to be the person who gives comfort, or do you receive comfort, or does it work both ways?

2. EXPLORATION, PLAY, JOY

As a child:

What did you think was fun, exciting, and entertaining?

What was one of your greatest experiences?

What did you associate with fun and excitement?

How did you spend your time?

Today:

What is your idea of having a good time?

What are your most important interests?

What do you do in your spare time?

Who would be a good person to have an experience or an outing with – partner, family, friends?

What would you really like to do – and with whom – if you could disregard money and commitments; if, for instance, you won the lottery or received an unexpected inheritance?

3. THE EXPERIENCE OF LOSS

As a child:

Did you experience any great losses or separations?

If so, how did you react? Did you cry? Did you grieve?

Did you talk to a comforting person about your feelings? Did you withdraw into yourself?

Have you ever run away from home? Or left your home without telling your parents where you were?

Today:

What have been the most difficult losses in your adult life? Did you lose anyone; did you have a divorce, fall out with friends, or with someone in the workplace?

How have you reacted to loss?

Which losses do you fear the most and how do you think you will react if they occur?

How easy is it for you to express your feelings when you feel disappointed or let down?

4. THE SMALL AND THE LARGE COGWHEEL

As a child:

What happened when you were angry or sad?

Who took those feelings seriously and listened to you?

Did you throw tantrums? If yes, what triggered them?

Were you able to say no to things you did not wish to do?

Could you ask for what you wanted and expect to be heard?

Today:

Describe an event or a story where you were angry.

What happened? What did you do?

If a friend or your partner does something to hurt you, how do you react? By outspoken anger, fury, sobbing, secret revenge, feeling miserable without doing anything?

Can you ask those who are closest to you for what you want?

Do you sometimes feel abandoned or let down? How do you react in this situation?

Have you ever had problems with aggression? Have you ever had broken relationships?

Do you ever feel compelled to do something or do you feel used or abused by other people especially those who are near to you?

5. OLD AND NEW HISTORY

As a child:

Describe a happy and unhappy childhood memory.

Draw a picture of yourself and your family as you would have seen it as a five-year-old and as a ten-year-old.

How would you have described a family event, such as, for instance, a holiday, Christmas, a birthday, or a funeral?

Today:

Take some photos of yourself and your family and talk about them. Talk about your hopes and dreams for the future for you and your family. Talk about how you think about yourself. Are you a person "who would prefer not to think and talk about yourself," or are you the type "who cannot stop thinking and talking about yourself?"

Inspired by *The Adult Attachment Interview* by Mary Maine and Jeremy Holmes.

AMERICAN
ICONS
AMSTERDAM

2 5. SEP. 1971

RELIEFS EN BRONZE D'ÉTRURIE

GLYPTOTHÈQUE
NY CARLSBERG

90

NEDERLAND
ERK

VESTIENDEBOEK
THE
B·I·G
FOOL

ACKNOWLEDGING INTIMACY
IN OUR DAILY LIVES

By now, it is no secret that to us that the recipe for a vibrant couple and family relationship is the acknowledging intimacy. In this chapter, we will take an in-depth look at what acknowledging intimacy is and what it means to live with or without this quality. Furthermore, we will focus on how we show acknowledging intimacy when we are with those we love.

Sharing acknowledging intimacy quite simply means that we are able to feel more authentically ourselves in an unambiguous way, and that we are able to be more aware of what goes on in the minds and souls of other people. For many reasons, we are not always equally ready to join in this "dance" with our children or partner. But don't panic; nobody is able at any given time to offer a 100% intimacy or acknowledgement. That is the human condition!

Sharing acknowledging intimacy can happen automatically and unconsciously, but the point here is that we can also begin to be more intentional and conscious about showing acknowledging intimacy. It is not difficult to talk, write, and read about the importance of being present and close in relationships. What is much more difficult is to practise what we preach – especially so when the music is playing louder and we are feeling insecure.

Acknowledging intimacy cannot be pigeonholed as a method, a set of skills, or a new kind of consciousness, as this new way of being in the world includes aspects of all these – a way of being which we, as parents, can choose to take an interest in.

HAUNTING OLD MOODS

Thomas and Stine are in their thirties and have just become parents. Their daughter, Louise, has turned their daily routines upside down. They are attempting to find a workable eating and sleeping pattern for Louise and the breast-feeding is going well. However, in certain situations, Thomas has difficulties with his new identity as a father. He cannot cope when Louise cries after being fed and changed. She is then supposed to have a quiet time with him while

Stine tries to get some sleep. Thomas tries in every possible way to comfort her and walks around with her in his arms. But to no avail, and Louise continues crying. Thomas reacts by falling into a bad mood; he gets annoyed and almost angry. By now, he thinks that Louise is being unreasonable. He feels inadequate and powerless and resorts to waking up Stine because she is, apparently, the only person who can comfort Louise. Thomas feels that this affects Stine. She wishes he would do his fair share so that she could get some rest. Thomas becomes sad and withdraws, and Stine also becomes a little depressed. Getting the daily routines to work takes almost all their energy and the emotional distance between them increases.

At one point, Stine tells Thomas that she well understands how difficult it is when he is unable to comfort Louise. She would like to talk about this because she becomes sad as well as anxious when she sees how annoyed Thomas gets with Louise and herself. This emphasizes Stine's feeling that she is left to her own devices. The atmosphere reminds her of her father and the years when she was alone with him and completely at the mercy of his moods.

Thomas realizes that they have to talk about this, and he tells her that he cannot handle Louise's crying. It gives him a feeling of powerlessness and he feels moody, like he did when he was a child. His mother was sometimes even sadder than he was, and she could not contain him and his feelings. Probably, Thomas did not learn to be confident about his own feelings, just like now, where he is not very confident at containing Louise's emotions.

Thomas thinks that his mother had a very difficult time when he was sad, and that perhaps she felt guilty because she wanted a divorce. He also remembers his mother telling him that his grandmother could not bear it when she cried as a child. Thomas is relieved when talking to Stine about these generational issues that are difficult to come to grips with.

Stine says that it affects her a lot when Thomas gets annoyed. She becomes anxious and nervous and gets palpitations. At this point, she gets nervous and anxious when Louise begins to cry. Because she fears the effect of Thomas's exasperation, Stine quickly takes Louise, goes to the bedroom, and closes the door in order to get some quiet time with the infant. She is better at handling things on her own and she prefers doing it alone in a state of calm, rather than involving Thomas and creating a stressed agitated atmosphere. In these situations, it does not occur to Stine that they could help and support each other. Quite the opposite; she feels that she will take care of Louise herself.

When Thomas and Stine have discussed the issues under-lying the ways they react, it becomes clear that these are not recent. These issues are not the result of just having had a baby, but have been amplified by the new situation they each experience on becoming parents. They now also have a clearer understanding of the fact that they can try to help each other move on with the issues that are problems for them as individuals. For instance, Thomas now feels that it is great that Stine knows about his struggle and that she would like to help him overcome his frustration when Louise cries. Thomas is well aware that it is not particularly helpful to Louise, or to Stine or himself, that he gets more and more stressed in these situations. Stine also thinks it is nice that Thomas knows how she feels about wanting to take care of things herself, that she has problems asking for help and telling people how she feels. Of course, Stine would like to get to the point where they can help each other instead of her doing most of the work. The effect of this will be that they each feel less lonely and can also support each other in being there for Louise when she feels sad.

Living in acknowledging intimacy as an adult means:

- that I can see your world through your eyes while also seeing my own world;

- that I can empathize with your point of view or your experience without agreeing with you and without needing to experience the situation exactly as you do;

- that I can sense other people's thoughts and emotions while being aware of my own;

- that I can move into your world without losing myself;

- that I can be in all kinds of relationships in a reflective and creative way;

- that I do not have problems maintaining close relationships.

In our view, children have two central capacities, which can be developed in the best possible way through the experience of acknowledging intimacy with parents and other significant adults. These two capacities are:

- the ability to regulate emotions;

- the ability to handle strain and stress.

These two abilities are key to ensuring the child's robustness and continued emotional and intellectual development.

THE ART OF CALMING YOURSELF DOWN

A child developing normally with a secure attachment pattern needs parents as a necessary "scaffolding function". The child will become less and less dependent on this function as he or she becomes better at regulating emotions and controlling spontaneous impulses (the psychological term is "affect regulation"). It is these two important abilities that are central to ensuring the development of the robust mental skills needed to tackle strain and challenges, as well as to tackle everyday interaction with other children and adults. To a great extent, a child's journey in learning to regulate his or her emotions and impulses depends on how well we parents are able to match his or her emotions. This means the extent to which we are capable of sharing our child's emotions and needs without inundating him or her with our own anxiety, annoyance, etc. Later, the child continues to develop his or her affect regulation in the classroom at school and playing with other children. Essentially, the challenge to learn to regulate our emotions and impulses continues throughout our lives.

When we interact with others, particularly in close relationships, we are constantly working towards maintaining a good balance in our emotional lives. It will come as no surprise that the ability we have to create harmony and balance as adults is directly linked to the skills we acquired in our early childhood and the opportunities we had to practise these skills later on.

There is only one way to learn this regulation: learning by doing. It may sound a little harsh, but there seems to be no other way forward. When we, as a couple, stay connected when strong feelings are involved, and we can both show that we can contain these feelings, our children learn from the process. They become conscious of the fact that they do not need to be alone with feelings and that there is hope for resolution or closure, for a way out even from the most chaotic and frightening scenarios. This process gives children a liberating and amazing feeling of relief that it is possible to restore a normal life. In other words, we can have experiences that feel like the end of the world and still survive together!

COMPLETE AND INCOMPLETE AFFECT REGULATION

Agnete and Mie are playing a game of cards. They both win and lose. However, their ways of tackling the situation when they lose differ. Every time Agnete loses, she becomes a little cross and moody. Still, she is soon ready for another game. However, when Mie loses, there is a strong reaction. Tears come to her eyes, she gets angry, and does not feel like playing any more. After some time, Mie can be persuaded to play another game.

THE MARSHMALLOW TEST

A very interesting, simple, and safe way of testing a child's capacity for self-regulation is the marshmallow test. It was first applied to a group of children between the ages of five and six. Their development of abilities and social functions was then monitored until they were fifteen years old. The test quite simply consists in asking a child to sit in front of a marshmallow. The child is then told that if he or she is able to refrain from eating the marshmallow when the adult leaves the room for a brief time, then he or she will get two marshmallows when the adult returns. What emerged was that the child who can "control him- or herself" and withstand the urge to gobble the marshmallow will, in later life, score highly when tested on social, relationship, and intellectual functions! This is a simple test that reveals the significance of self-regulation for healthy child development.

STRESS IS POISON TO CHILDREN

The capacity to manage stress is necessary if we are to become able to explore and rise to life's challenges. Stress that is predictable and more frequent or sustained can arrest the development of a child's brain and even kill brain cells. Looking at things from the perspective of stress can help us to understand the development of the insecurely attached child, who becomes more vulnerable than the securely attached resilient child.

Children who do not experience a restoration of the connection after episodes on the small cogwheel, in the shame trap, or under unexpected emotional strain will be stressed. When children have such a continual overload of stress on their nervous system, the result is that later on they will experience difficulty in finding appropriate ways to respond to pressure.

In these situations, children need something that we parents should always be able to provide: restoration. What these children need most is that parents move on to the large cogwheel, continue interacting, and restore a good and safe atmosphere. This is especially relevant when things are at their worst, when we parents feel we cannot cope. In order to break the vicious circle, we need to be able to sense and regulate our own affect and stress levels and match them with those experienced by our partner and children. This not only reduces stress, it also gives we parents valuable experience and helps our children to learn mastering stress in similar situations.

THE ART OF GETTING BY

The resilient child is a wonderfully inclusive concept: a child who can manage most of life's challenges in a satisfactory way – not a "Teflon child", on whom nothing makes any impression. No, we want a child who is capable of facing and overcoming difficult times and emerging the stronger for it together with others. This is no simple task.

What we are suggesting here is that we can equip ourselves as parents by building on evidence-based knowledge that is not based on superstition, personal beliefs, or fashionable ideas about what is good for our children.

PICNIC ANYWAY!

Jens and Minna have decided that the family, including Villads, three, and Oscar, nine, will be going on a picnic in the forest in the morning. Oscar does not think this is a good idea.

Jens tells him that they are going to go for a walk in the nice weather to get some fresh air. He attempts to persuade Oscar to put on his clothes and convince him that he should come along. Oscar does not want to go; he cries, gets moody and angry, and goes to his room.

Jens discusses the incident with Minna as to how they can get back on track and still have a good day. Minna listens to Jens' impatience and annoyance with Oscar and supports his effort to listen to Oscar's wishes instead of continuing to persuade him.

Jens goes to Oscar's room. Oscar has calmed down. Jens asks him what he would like to do. At the beginning of the conversation, it is a little difficult for Oscar to express what he wants to do. At some point, however, it nevertheless becomes clear. He would like to go into the garden and chop wood with Jens and later play a game of Monopoly. Jens mirrors what Oscar just said, and checks if that is what he wants to do. Oscar says yes. Then Jens says that now he understands. He, too, wants to go into the garden and later play a game with Oscar.

Then Jens says that he would also like to do some other specific and important things with Oscar during the weekend. Oscar is now very attentive. He is not usually as attentive as he is right now.

Jens tells Oscar that he would like to go on a picnic in the forest with him, Minna, and Villads. This could well be at some other time than first suggested. Jens asks Oscar if he understands and he nods. Oscar now also wants to go to the forest at some time, and Jens notices that Oscar seems surprised by the fact that now he wants to come along for the picnic. Oscar is now very open and happy and brightens up. His sense of security, connection, and calm has been restored.

The family goes to the forest and talk about how they all need to be understood, especially when there are disagreements between parents and children or communication problems with someone you love. They discuss how it is a very good idea to be open towards each other's wishes, even if these do not correspond to one's own.

For the rest of the weekend there is a very good atmosphere and energy in the family. Oscar has more energy to take care of his younger brother than normally, and he makes the tomato sauce for the pasta dish for dinner. Jens and Minna also feel much better because they have resolved a critical situation in a really good and effective way. Jens was able to stay on the large cogwheel and get Oscar on board.

CODEWORD: RESTORATION

When our children do not develop their own ability to effectively regulate the intensity of their emotions when under strain, one of the reasons is that we parents have not been good enough at changing gears from the small to the large cogwheel and, thus, restoring a connection and a good atmosphere. According to many researchers, it is precisely the lack of ability to match the other person's wavelength and provide a safe harbour that can, in the long run, cause the development of psychological problems. Another way to say this is that during our childhood we developed too many survival strategies and too few mastery skills.

Typically, it is when we are in our closest relationships that situations occur where restoration is frequently needed. For this reason, it makes very good sense to highlight how children thrive in close relationships, because this is certainly where "the action is"!

Isolated episodes of noisy dogfights, even if your child will probably be in shock as a result of them, are not the main problem. Lasting damage occurs when there is a repeated pattern of conflicts and flaring tempers, after which the connection is not restored. Repeated restoration on the large cogwheel teaches children how to get back on track. The repeated pattern, its style, and the tone created in the process of changing gears from the small to the large cogwheel are important to the child! It is also essential that we, as parents, dare to work with the confident hope that emotional or conflicting ups and downs can all be overcome with curiosity, imagination, humour, and acknowledging intimacy. We parents can, therefore, solve our problems by developing our own resilience while we work on these problems.

These are the normal and natural processes that we consider to be most important. It is through these processes that we parents best support our child's brain development. We are quite convinced that all this work can be done in the safest possible way, with the maximum benefit for all of us, when we parents offer each other support to stay on, or return to, the large cogwheel. We need to model this for our children.

THE ADVANCED TEST FOR PARENTS – LIFE ON THE LARGE COGWHEEL

Our clear recommendation is not to hesitate one second before getting up on the bike and oiling the gears. Many of us have no problem with changing gears in conflicts in the workplace or with friends. However, when conflicts arise in close relationships, it is different. Here, changing gears from the small to the large cogwheel may feel very painful, as we well know. The process may feel awkward and wrong, like the first few times we try a new skill. In addition, there may be strong conflicting feelings at play.

- It may feel difficult having to stretch oneself to the point of understanding and feeling the other person while just being curious and "not knowing".
  (If we wind back the film to the time when Jens and Minna were going on a picnic, Jens might be frustrated

and think: *What the hell can I do if Oscar does not want to come? It cannot be right that he should spoil the whole weekend!*)

- It can feel like risking being "engulfed" by any other person's process, so much so that we can become afraid of not being able to return to our own world again. (Jens might think: *And what about next time? Then he will just throw a tantrum if he does not want to go to school.*)

- It may feel like a waste of time and can be associated with feelings of insecurity, vulnerability, and confusion if we are expected only to listen and be present in an unhurried way so that things can unfold at their pace. (Jens might think: *It is a waste of time to listen to what Oscar has to tell. It is time to go on the picnic now.*)

We might in fact prefer to be in our "familiar hell", the small cogwheel, as opposed to moving into the "unfamiliar paradise", because we have tried the unfamiliar before and it did not work out very well! The reason is that when we try to develop some new quality, which we did not establish as children, we bump into some of the forgotten, hurtful, and painful experiences of childhood. In fact, we encounter precisely those experiences that stopped us from learning all the good and useful things about being able to enjoy the acknowledging intimacy with one another.

Every time there is an episode involving us on the small cogwheel, the responsibility is our own. The damage is done – we have done it again – and the result is distance and frustration, tears or anger, felt by you, your child, or your partner. You or your partner has the responsibility for initiating an Acknowledging Dialogue, which could begin as follows:

I got very angry – I am sorry about that – I understand that you were frightened and sad . . .

I would like to discuss this in an appropriate way – are you ready for that now, or should we . . .

At this point, it is your responsibility to keep the momentum going, return to the scene of the episode, change gears, and together get the chain back on to the large cogwheel with the person who was there when it jumped off. We hope that you, like us, will find that there are many good reasons to start an Acknowledging Dialogue, even if it feels difficult. Remember that when you and your partner choose to challenge yourselves and each other for the benefit and joy of your child, then you will need a plentiful supply of patience and flexibility. During your first attempts, you might feel doubtful and awkward. New conflicts or power struggles about this issue can even be waiting to happen.

Statements such as: *Come on . . . it cannot be as difficult as all that* and *We agreed to . . .* are "forbidden".

Your child probably has also become quite used to some of your reactions when on the small cogwheel. When you begin to change, your child needs a little extra time, patience, and consideration in order to "catch up". Your child has already developed his or her own style, which you need to acknowledge, even if you now believe that you can offer quite a different perspective.

You will begin to experience that you can change. Furthermore, these changes may confirm to you the certainty that this is precisely what your child or your partner needs. Why? Because they (surprise surprise!) have the same need that you have! You are not in doubt when you meet your partner and he or she offers acknowledgement and intimacy: you begin to feel good, experience a burst of energy, your heart beats faster, and you feel heard and seen as the person you are. As a result you feel like giving as well as receiving more!

This seems like a major change – and we believe that it is: beginning to understand parenthood as a new opportunity to gain knowledge about your child, yourself, and each other.

DEVELOPMENT OF ACKNOWLEDGING INTIMACY

From birth, your child begins to develop a capacity for acknowledging intimacy – a process that accelerates until the age of seven and continues to do so for the rest of his or her life – at a reduced pace!

If we empathize with our child's world while still being in our own, the child learns to identify with our world and, later, its own. Our child can, for example, learn to pay attention and maintain his or her focus in a variety of situations when we parents draw his or her attention to certain things we see. At a later stage, we parents can reveal more of ourselves, sharing our thoughts and emotions. We do not need to share everything, but in relation with our child we should share on a "need to know" basis.

Children develop acknowledging intimacy when we:

- give them room and space to repeat actions;
- give them room to begin to think about their own thought processes;
- give them permission to experience and tolerate feelings of closeness as well as separation;
- give them the opportunity to reflect on emotional experiences;
- when we, as adults, are able to understand and empathize with our child and ourselves simultaneously and our child is so calm and confident that he or she is able to experience it.

. . . we are on a picnic in the forest with our child, who has just learnt to walk. We follow at the child's pace, look at the flowers, the leaves, and the birds through the eyes of the child. We talk to the child and name the things we see and the things the child sees . . .

As with many other aspects of life, our ability to create acknowledging intimacy improves the more we practise. Our development is affected in several ways. We become better at being close to other people while also developing a greater ability to notice our own thoughts and feelings.

Inspired by Daniel Stern, we shall, in the following pages, describe the connection between the developmental steps which we can observe and feel in our child. We shall also describe the invisible brain development, and, finally, look at how precisely acknowledging intimacy provides opportunities to meet our child's needs.

1. THE FIRST SLOW DANCE –
FROM BIRTH TO THE AGE OF THREE MONTHS

INTERACTION

The relationship between mother and infant is a biological entity that involves a kind of "substance dependence". Even short separations of a few minutes can create physiological and psychological "withdrawal symptoms" in the infant, as well as in the parent. A premature separation is an enormous strain on your child, and it arrests the growth of the brain.

Psychologically, physiologically, and in terms of brain development, your infant is completely dependent on your being close. You are in the process of getting to know another human being, and all the events that take place between you are preparations for his or her development into a mature individual. The infant has a growing desire to explore and make contact, a capacity to be comforted, and to regulate his or her affect. The infant is already able to "feel felt". He or she imitates your grimaces and is able to withdraw from contact. The connection, the interaction, and the intimacy are formed during the first few days of life. It is a wonderful time. You and your partner are on cloud nine, but for the time being there is room for only one person at a time to be with your infant. However, soon there will be nappies to change and some feeding to do, and your different beliefs about child rearing will start to emerge.

Your infant's right brain hemisphere is in the middle of a growth spurt. Other parts of the brain are already active and function well with the parts that mediate the body's developing sensations and reactions to external stimulation, such as touch, sight, warmth, food, sound, and movements. All these responses make up the way the infant begins to process sensations, impressions, emotions, and defence reactions, which need a response and even to be "kick started" by we parents. During the first eight weeks, it is especially sight and skin contact, as well as the smell function, that stimulate the growth of the brain. The child's entire system is totally dependent on our presence, responsiveness, and regulation. It is through our active intervention and gentle attentive intimacy that the brain's further growth is stimulated and regulated. The brain's vision centres are active and drive a significant part of the infant's contact function.

Your acknowledging intimacy could look like:
- offering plenty of skin-to-skin contact. Off with your clothes!;
- offering plenty of eye contact on the infant's terms;
- imitating your infant's sounds and movements, in particular with your facial expressions;
- offering rhythm with sound, your voice, your movements, etc.;
- being aware of your infant's rhythm and need for stimulation, breaks, cradling, comfort, and breast feeding;
- being present, playful, and spontaneous;
- describing your and your infant's behaviour out loud with words and movements;
- seeing your infant as a separate person in his or her own right, with reasons for doing what he or she does;
- restoring normality after accidental happenings that can be stressful for your child;
- giving your partner the opportunity to enjoy your time together with your infant and giving yourself the same opportunity to enjoy when your partner spends time with your infant.

2. THE RHYTHM OF THE DANCE INCREASES FROM THREE TO SEVEN MONTHS

INTERACTION

You and your child now have a strong bond where she clearly recognizes you and reacts to your absence. She can maintain contact and begin to play with her body and find toys whose rhythm and repetition are attractive and joyful. You imitate her facial expressions and movements and name out loud the things she plays with. She now has a greater ability to express and share joy and frustration. She is able to sustain to a certain extent an expectation that something will happen. She can deal better with frustration, and begins to regulate affect, emotions, and stress.

Her growth spurt has now reached the areas in the brain which process information about facial expressions, attention, and physical pleasure; she is beginning to understand that things can exist without needing to see them.

Your acknowledging intimacy could consist of:
- mirroring her facial expressions;
- waiting for your child's initiative;
- being reliable;
- taking turns in playing and other activities;
- doing things together;
- doing something with repetition and something with variation;
- imitating, repeating, beginning "finger language" and naming of things, using body language
- restoring normality after accidental happenings that might be stressful to the child;
- giving your partner the opportunity to watch and occasionally participate in your interaction with your child and vice versa.

3. AGREEMENTS AND DISAGREEMENTS ABOUT THE DANCE – FROM EIGHT TO FIFTEEN MONTHS

INTERACTIVE UNDERSTANDING

You and your child now have a firm bond. He begins to experiment with the limits of his behaviour. In his present repertoire of interaction he is, however, completely dependent on your acknowledging intimacy while developing an interactive understanding. His sky-high but inconsistent levels of curiosity and joy need your support and clear communication. Saying no and setting boundaries provide for intense training in impulse control for all three of you. When frustration is the response to your boundary setting, it is your important task as a parent to restore the acknowledging intimacy – partly because your child expects you to do so, partly because your child relies on you to do so, partly because he cannot yet do so himself. All your emotional efforts when seeking and finding ways to establish a new understanding with your child are critical for brain development.

The use of language is a possibility, but his language is still not fully understandable. At this stage, misunderstanding and being misunderstood are extremely important. When children act on unclear messages, it creates confusion and elicits strong feelings when they fail. This can lead, for instance, to withdrawal, hostility, and rejection or over-protective behaviour. Your adult explanations might, at this stage, be too complex for him, and you might end up manipulating him with your unclear questions.

The child's brain is developing rapidly and the connections between the various parts of the brain are consolidating. He can now begin to look forward to events in the future. He is now more flexible, is able to maintain attention for longer periods of time, and has a repertoire of a variety of responses and may be including words. In short, he is now more in control of his emotions and bodily sensations. He is immersed in the development of his senses and intuitive understanding of other people and himself. The core elements of the acknowledging intimacy are now in place!

Your acknowledging intimacy could be characterized by:
- emotional matching;
- non-verbal communication with eye contact and mimicry;
- wordless contact;
- taking the initiative when sharing emotions;
- making yourself available;
- coherent, predictable, and clear communication;
- taking the initiative to play new games;
- introducing give and take games;
- developing already established games;
- imitating your child's pointing while you name those actions and things that have caught your child's interest;
- restoring normality after accidental happenings that might be stressful to the child;
- together with your partner, ensure there is space to develop interactive understanding verbally and non-verbally with your child.

4. THE WORDS BECOME SENTENCES THAT FORM THE DANCE - FROM SIXTEEN MONTHS TO THREE YEARS

CONVERSATION

There are important changes during this stage of development. Disconnected phrases are gradually formed into coherent sentences and you can now have a conversation. Children want to be understood in what they say, as they struggle to learn their language. The way the children see the world informs the way they set their agenda at this stage: "I want wine gum now!"

This stage has inappropriately been called the defiant, or the assertive, age. But children only become defiant if we become defiant! Your child has passed through the first stages in good shape and is able to handle extremely high levels of joy, energy, curiosity, and stress, all experienced with a great appetite for life!

The growth spurt continues in your child's brain. In addition to the explosion of language, the control centres for emotion and motor activity are also developing fast.

Your acknowledging intimacy could look as follows:
- mirroring what your child says;
- savouring your child's words;
- creating old and new meanings of language together;
- making sure there are verbal connections between experiences and emotions;
- making room for your child's emerging story;
- restoring normality after accidental happenings that might be stressful to the child;
- making room for conversations with your child.

5. STORIES ABOUT THE DANCE YESTERDAY AND TOMORROW WHILE WE ARE DANCING – FROM THREE YEARS ON

INTERACTIVE CREATION AND COHESION

Your child has started to develop all the mental and physical functions, but has not yet mastered them. You support your child in becoming still more conscious of herself and the surrounding world. Her brain has now entered a calm phase of development leading up to the next growth spurt, which will begin at the onset of puberty. The developed sections of the brain are trained, organized, and reorganized. This means that she feels even more robust and becomes even better at regulating her feelings and handling strain and stress.

In her fourth year, the child develops an understanding of how language, affect, and communication are connected. The translation of experiences into language is activated by her inner dialogues, thoughts, and stories.

Your acknowledging intimacy could look as follows:
- helping your child story her experience in a constructive way;
- supporting your child in talking about emotional aspects of her experience;
- supporting your child's ability to restore their own emotional balance;
- restoring normality after accidental happenings that might be stressful to the child;
- listening to and acknowledging your child expressing her strong will – while you stay calmly on the large cogwheel;
- creating colourful and coherent stories with your child and your partner together.

6. TEN STANDARD DANCES WOULD NOT BE ENOUGH – FROM SEVEN YEARS AND ONWARDS

SUMMA SUMMARUM

Mastery of all these early dances lays the foundation for the energy for the continued journey through youth and adult life – energy for us as well as our relationships. We have reason to believe that these developmental stages are inextricably connected with our ongoing brain development. When we have the ability to sense another person's point of view as well as understanding our own position, then we are able to create, as well as participate in, the acknowledging intimacy – mentalizing – for the joy and satisfaction of ourselves, our relationships, and our brains.

The growth spurt of puberty happens on physical and behavioural levels as well as in the brain. Often, we experience rollercoaster rides from childlike to adult behaviour and back again, coming and going like unpredictable spring rain.

We will be asked to dance still more demanding and difficult dances, where our personal and parental boundaries will be stretched, often to our limits, and sometimes beyond them.

At this stage, the brain is undergoing the last major phase of reorganization and this characterizes puberty. This may explain much of the passing behaviour that occurs until the brain is fully developed. At this stage, it is advantageous to be two or more people in order to maintain an emotional focus on interactive understanding, set limits, negotiate roles, and consistently initiate gear changes to the large cogwheel. Remember that when you go off on the small cogwheel, you should first turn to your partner and not to your child. It then follows that you can be on the large cogwheel when you need to be available for the process of solving problems in the encounters with your teenager.

Your acknowledging intimacy with older children could involve the following characteristics:
- being playful and spontaneous;
- being present in a supportive way, allowing your teenager to have his or her own feelings and talking about how you experience this;
- listening attentively, "tell . . ." and "tell me more . . .", then saying what you think;
- being clear and setting down limits while you are on the large cogwheel;
- thinking out loud, finding connections, and creating new opportunities together.

During the reading of this book, parents of older children may have often thought, like us: *Hey, I did something else in that situation. I did what I could and that corresponded to my knowledge at the time.* To those of you thinking like this, we wish to say (as we have said to ourselves and to our older and adult children): *That is fine! All our experience tells us that it is possible to start out from here as well, and that it always pays off when we decide to change our ways with our children, grandchildren, ourselves, and in our relationships.*

Happy dancing!

REFLECTIONS

1. Think of an earlier time where you have experienced being seen as the person you were. Tell this story to your partner, who listens closely and with acknowledgment. Then reverse the roles , so that your partner tells his or her story of similar experiences.

2. Think of a situation in your present family where you were not acknowledged, where you experienced not being seen and heard as the person you are. Tell this story to your partner, who listens carefully and with acknowledgement. Then your partner shares what he or she thought and felt while you told your story . . .

3. Think of a new or recent experience with your child where you felt you were "not available". What happened? What did you do? How did your child react? How did you react? How did you bring/not bring closure to the situation? Looking back, what are your thoughts, what could you have done that would have been more appropriate? Tell your partner, who listens and mirrors with acknowledgement.
   You conclude the process with a summary and, possibly, a decision about one new type of behaviour you would like to begin to practise. You could also think about what your partner could do to make it easier for you to commit yourself to the change.

4. Think about a stressful situation for you and your child/ family. Tell your partner about your experience, while he or she listens and mirrors in an acknowledging way. What does this remind you of? Then reverse the roles.

5. Next time your child reacts in a way that aggravates you, try to notice your own reaction. Try to stretch and contain the emotion while keeping the contact with your child. Observe, mirror, and follow up. When the communication is open, you share what you experience: *When you shout, then I feel. . .*

VIKTOR IV
AMERICAN
IKONS
AMSTERDAM

ETOILE — 14.5. 1970

NEDERLAND
juiste

← 40 stone BALK. ENDS

Greek
Relief
pattern

79

DER TIENDE BOEK
* PLEASE DO *
NOT

THE ACKNOWLEDGING DIALOGUE

In the previous chapters, we have discussed how we can develop acknowledging intimacy, and how our neurobiological development is directly influenced by acknowledging intimacy. In this chapter, we will try to look at the ways and means we can use in order to create and achieve acknowledging intimacy between us as partners. We shall also look at how this affects our children and how we, in a joint effort with our children, can develop an explicit acknowledging intimacy.

The tool we use is called the Acknowledging Dialogue. To us, this opens up an extremely efficient and exciting pathway to the development of deeper, more enduring, and generous relationships. The Acknowledging Dialogue is, first and foremost, a way of communicating which opens up a new connection and empathy. This dialogue is inspired by Active Listening and Imago Relationship Therapy.

We have chosen to call the tool the Acknowledging Dialogue because, to our way of thinking, acknowledgement is a central concept. In this context, acknowledgement means a way of being which enables us to put ourselves in our partner's shoes and see the world through our partner's eyes. In addition, acknowledgement includes the ability to respect the fact that our partner may see the world differently from us. As we have mentioned, difference does not equal deficit.

Acknowledgement has an amazing effect. It supports and promotes a lot of positive development. When we are acknowledged by our partner, we feel seen, heard, understood, and respected for the person we are. This gives us confidence and security – crucial elements in a process where our partner dares to change and where we and our child develop and express ourselves confidently.

Being in the Acknowledging Dialogue is not just a temporary process. When it has become second nature, this way of thinking and being can lead to a completely new way of being together, not just as a couple, but also with our children, friends, and colleagues. The Acknowledging Dialogue is not an end in itself: it is a pathway to acknowledging intimacy.

We have derived much pleasure from this dialogue. In pedagogical terms, it is easily accessible and, if you intend to change old patterns that create distance between you, it is immediately effective. It is easy to learn, and when you use it, you discover that it has several deeper layers. However, in order to get used to the slow pace and tight structure that are the basic rules of the first stages of the Acknowledging Dialogue, a commitment to the process is necessary.

The Acknowledging Dialogue offers the opportunity to:

- recreate confidence and curiosity;
- develop both participants' understanding of themselves and each other;
- dissolve conflicts and power struggles;
- create acknowledging intimacy;
- enable access to childhood memories and letting the untold stories unfold and create new meaning;
- reveal our survival strategies so we become aware of our small cogwheel and the change of gears.

An extremely important point is that once we have become confident using the Acknowledging Dialogue, it can be applied anywhere by anybody with and without the assistance of professionals. The Acknowledging Dialogue has a fixed structure with clear and simple rules, as well as its own particular process. With a little practice, the Acknowledging Dialogue can develop into a way of being in the world, a basic approach to the ways in which we share our thoughts and resolve our differences.

We would like to give you the opportunity to try out the Acknowledging Dialogue with your partner. It is one thing to hear and read about it, but experiencing the process will give you a completely different point of view. The process is like all other types of learning – it should be tried out and it should be practised. It is just like skiing: you have to practise before you can enjoy the fun and before you can decide if skiing is for you. So get going! When you have tried to go through the three steps of the Acknowledging Dialogue a few times, you will already know much more about how you can use the process on a daily basis.

You can see an example of the Acknowledging Dialogue on the homepage www.denlevendefamilie.dk

There is a "set-up" phase to the Acknowledging Dialogue, where you invite your partner to a dialogue. Then you make agreements about when and where you want to have the dialogue and what you want to talk about. The prelude is also about who starts out telling a personal story and who listens. You should focus on a theme which concerns you – a theme which you would like to say something about, or know more about, and which preoccupies the two of you in your relationship or in your roles as parents. It is not something you do while you are washing up, or in the middle of a quarrel.

If you do choose to start talking about a frustrating situation, it is important that you focus on something that you or your partner is doing, rather than on a character trait that you cannot change. Whether you criticize yourself or you are criticized by others, a criticism of your personality will have greater negative impact than if the criticism is focused on actions and behaviours that you can change. There is a difference between what we do and who we are.

THE PROCESS OF THE ACKNOWLEDGING DIALOGUE

EYE CONTACT

The two participants in the Acknowledging Dialogue should sit facing each other. In this way, you try to create a magical distance. The seating arrangement needs to facilitate the sense of a special contact and physical presence reminiscent of times where we were held by our parents' gaze and closeness. Anyone who has held an infant knows that there is a special distance where there is good opportunity for deep and intimate eye contact.

As parents, we automatically adjust head, hands, and arms to this magical distance where child and adult can rest in each others' gaze and experience an intense physical calm. In the same way, we can, as adults, sit in front of each other, have deep eye contact, and experience a profound sense of security.

At times like this, the brain enters the game on an unconscious level. This wordless eye contact activates brain processes that are nurturing and which generate a deep mutual calm and joy. It is a worthwhile exercise, relearning to stay in close contact and find reassurance, especially when the eye contact is a challenge.

This particular position, where we face each other, activates many thoughts and emotions we may even feel awkward. This is quite natural. However, as we know, every new beginning is difficult. So don't give up. In time, this specific position will become a source of confidence and curiosity that will take the strain out of the situation. We might even begin to long for a couple of minutes of complete silence and deep eye contact with our partner.

In a fragile relationship, where a couple is not getting along, maintaining eye contact can be painful and almost impossible. It is for this reason the "setup" is so important, since it helps to repair and reinforce a new, as yet fragile, connection between two bruised partners.

People who have grown up with an insecure attachment pattern may, in general, have difficulty maintaining eye contact. However, in such situations, it will also be possible to heal old pain by consciously working with these difficult issues.

THE SPACE BETWEEN

When eye contact has been established, the time comes to investigate and feel the "space between" the partners, who are now sitting quite close, face to face. "The space between" is the shared space in which to work. However, it is also the space in which we live and breathe on a daily basis. "The space between" is everything we say and do together. Hence, our ways of interacting have a crucial role in determining whether the room is nice or unpleasant to be in. Even if one of the partners is at work and the other is at home, there is still a space – an invisible connection – between the partners.

When we meet a couple who are comfortable together, we know that it is because they have a special connection and it is this that makes it inspiring to be in their company. We feel the safe, vibrant space they share, a fertile field where love grows.

When we are unhappy together, the "space between" is no longer pleasant to inhabit – not for the couple or for the children who are also part of this space. An important lesson is to learn to protect this space through understanding that one cannot fill it with all kinds of negative feelings without serious consequences. The Acknowledging Dialogue can contribute to the creation of a healthy consciousness of the shared responsibility for this important intermediate space. In this way, this space can begin to flourish.

TAKING TURNS

In a dialogue there is someone who listens and someone who talks. You take turns talking and listening. If two people listen, then not much will be said. A prerequisite for hearing each other's story is the creation of a calm atmosphere. Telling his or her story sincerely and in full contact with the listener is a challenge for the storyteller. The storyteller invites the other person across the bridge, and the challenge is to keep the door open when the listener arrives. The challenge to the listener is to be 100% present for the storyteller by receiving the story as it is experienced by the storyteller – in other words, to put his or her own thoughts and emotions on hold. It is a challenge not to be distracted by your own thoughts and feelings. At the same time, however, it can also be a relief to know that all he or she has to do is to listen and mirror.

CROSSING THE BRIDGE

There is an invisible narrow bridge between you and your partner. You can take turns in leaving your safe harbour, walking on to the bridge, and crossing to the other person's door in order to be invited in to listen and understand what is going on in the other person's world. The storyteller "remains at home" and concentrates on telling his or her experiences, and the listener crosses the bridge in order to visit. We visit, so to speak, each other's reality. The bridge is an illustration of the contact and closeness we offer each other.

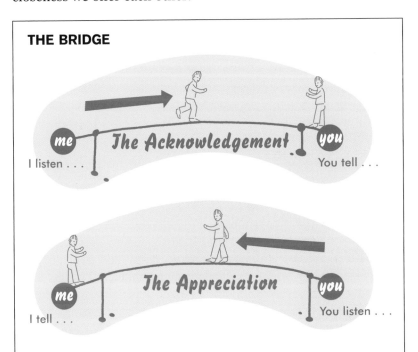

THE BRIDGE

The Acknowledgement

me — I listen . . .

you — You tell . . .

The Appreciation

me — I tell . . .

you — You listen . . .

The entire dialogue is based on the premise that the listener leaves his or her "own world" in order to cross over the bridge to his or her partner's world and hear and understand more about the partner. Here, the "bridge" will help us make contact. In order to listen to everything your partner has to say, you move across the bridge, which is so narrow that there is only room for one person at a time. Now you as well as the listener should take turns to leave your safe home ground, opening your door, walking on to the bridge, reach the other person's door, and being invited in. This is as if you visit each other's reality.

The bridge, which is a central element in the Acknowledging Dialogue, is an idea which can be used in very many ways by adults as well as children.

By training awareness in how to behave on this bridge, we train ourselves in knowing where we are in our communication. If we are completely committed to visiting in the other person's reality and leaving our own behind, then we are in an acknowledging intimacy. When we become secure in our position on the bridge, we can quickly feel when, for some reason, we run back to our own reality. We then have the opportunity to tell the other person that we did a "home run". Then we can return back across the bridge to the intimacy.

WHERE ON THE BRIDGE ARE YOU NOW, MOTHER?

Ida and her mother are on a constant collision course. They are, among other things, introduced to the idea of the bridge, which turns out to be a useful image for them both. It emerges that the mother has a very difficult time staying in her position on Ida's side of the bridge when Ida says how she feels. Hence, Ida has become very good at asking: "Where on the bridge are you now, mother?" Working on finding their positions on the bridge, it occurs to Ida that she is actually afraid of telling her mother about things that will make her sad. The mother is distressed to hear this. She was not aware of this at all. Likewise, she was unaware of the fact that she was not present and close in the way that Ida needed.

Moreover, the bridge is also an important idea in terms of demonstrating the difference between when we appreciate and praise or when we acknowledge those we love. When we appreciate and praise, we have an experience of an aspect of the other which pleases us or makes us proud. In this situation, we remain on our side of the bridge and invite the person we appreciate or praise to our own world in order to tell him or her what we, on our side of the bridge, appreciate and are proud of in the other person.

On the other hand, acknowledgement is about leaving "my world" and crossing the bridge in order to hear and understand more about the other person's world, whether it is positive or negative. The important thing is to be motivated to want to hear and understand the other person's experience on their side of the bridge.

That may all be very well, but is it not a little elaborate and contrived? Do I really have to go on a visit via a narrow little imaginary bridge? I know my husband through and through, don't I? Maybe, but if we want to, we can spend a lifetime exploring each other and discovering new insights, new perspectives, and new experiences with each other.

For this reason, we should try to bring our curiosity and openness along and cross the bridge to our partner in order to visit his or her innermost places, realities, and past in a new way. Likewise, our partner may pay us a visit.

One of the major challenges in crossing the bridge is the strong force that, from time to time, attempts to pull us back home to apparent safety. While we make great efforts listening to and visiting our partner, thoughts, emotions, and impulses will pop up that will make us want to "go home". When our partner begins to tell us something about which we have strong feelings, it becomes particularly difficult to put our thoughts on hold. When we begin an inner dialogue with our own opinions, this interior dialogue will "drown out" our partner's story and our impulse will be to run home.

The reason is that the listener always has a "yes, but . . ." animal on his or her shoulder, which constantly needs to defend itself. *Yes, but it was not like that,* or *Yes, but that was not what I said. Don't you think it was more like . . .,* or *Yes, but don't you think I was hurt as well?*

The "yes, but . . ." animal must be kept on a short leash by the person who listens. If the partner feels that the listener is not genuinely attentive, he or she will not dare to open up and be vulnerable.

It is not always easy to keep our "yes, but . . ." animal on a leash. Occasionally, an intense inner dialogue will be taking place in the listener's head about wanting to go home and defend him- or herself. This dialogue can be so disturbing that the listener is, in fact, unable to concentrate on or even hear what the partner is saying.

When the listener is out on the bridge, struggling to find out where he or she should be, it is evident to the partner that a struggle is going on. Due to the physical closeness, the eye contact, the intuitive sense of openness, our partner immediately senses if we are not genuinely present. Once we have opened up and begun to share our innermost experiences, it is very unpleasant to realize that the other person has gone "home".

When this happens, you just say, "Oops! I ran 'home' and now I am going back to you." Or something to that effect. It is important that you say it out loud when it happens, so your partner knows what is going on in your mind. Another reason for saying it aloud is that it helps you to develop your own awareness of where on the bridge you are standing – whether you are acknowledging, connected, or just pretending . . .

THE STRUCTURE OF THE ACKNOWLEDGING DIALOGUE

The Acknowledging Dialogue has a storyteller and a listener who go through three steps together:

STEP 1: MIRRORING
STEP 2: ACKNOWLEDGEMENT
STEP 3: EMPATHY

THE ACKNOWLEDGING DIALOGUE

The storyteller tells his or her story and the listener mirrors, makes a summary, acknowledges, and empathizes.

STEP 1: MIRRORING

The cornerstone of the Acknowledging Dialogue is a mirroring process, which, in efficient and simple ways, can open up our own

MIRRORING

This refers to a process where the listener performs a precise mirroring of the words of the storyteller's story.
Did I get everything you said . . .?
Was that what you said . . .?
Do you want to tell me more . . .?

SUMMARY

The listener summarizes what he or she has heard
Did I get the most important issues?

ACKNOWLEDGEMENT

This refers to a process whereby the listener affirms that the story that he or she have heard makes sense. The listener hears the story as if seeing the world through the storytellers eyes without necessarily agreeing.
I understand what you are saying and it makes sense that you would feel/think that way when you . . .?
Do you feel understood by me . . .?

EMPATHY

This refers to a process whereby the listener tunes into the feelings described in the story.
I imagine that what you must feel about this story is . . .
Is this what you feel and are there any other emotions . . .?

and our partner's eyes, ears, and heart in a completely new way. The purpose of the mirroring is to create a secure framework in which we can develop an understanding of each other's worlds and allow our authentic self to flourish in each other's presence. Mirroring, quite simply, means that the listener moves into the storyteller's world and mirrors by repeating what the storyteller says. This is a kind of active listening, where the listener exactly reflects the words of the storyteller's message. When the listener mirrors, it is important to do it as in as verbatim a way as possible. We may all feel as if we are repeating what we just heard when we use a variation of the exact wording, either because we cannot remember precisely what was said, or because we would like to show our partner that we have been reflecting on it and are not just repeating it verbatim. The whole point is to repeat it verbatim. If the listener does not do that, he or she will, by using his or her own words, anchor the story in his or her own world and not in the world of the storyteller.

Being mirrored gives the storyteller a peaceful feeling that is rare and a sense of being heard and understood in a very authentic way. By mirroring what our partner tells us, we attempt to learn our partner's language and, indirectly, also understand the thought processes behind the words. For this reason, mirroring is a particularly useful tool when practising putting "our own world" on hold for a while in order to be able to focus on listening to and understanding our partner's story. In other words, practising acknowledging intimacy.

If you are in doubt, just mirror the best way you can. When the mirroring is complete and you ask if you have heard what the storyteller was saying, then he or she will let you know if you got the gist of the story or not. When you mirror someone imprecisely, you actually help the storyteller to become even more clear and precise by prompting him or her to tell you the essence of the story again.

When you begin a mirroring process, you need to take your time. The quality of your listening will be an expression of the quality of your presence and connection. Every time you have mirrored, you ask your partner if this is what your partner said. Your partner's answer could be: *Yes, you got quite a lot*, or *well, nearly ... What I would also like you to hear is ...*

It is in this way that the exploration of the story and the mirroring continue without either partner interrupting each other until the storyteller feels that his or her frustration, problem, or experiences have been fully heard. Then the listener offers a summary of the story he or she has heard.

Both participants in the dialogue share the responsibility for not speaking for so long that the listener has trouble mirroring. As you work through the dialogue process, you will find your own rhythm, so that the storyteller does not overload the listener with words at any one time. It is also a question of practice, and occasionally you will experience that you are actually able to remember an increasing number of sentences. This ensures that the narrative will not be broken up too much.

The first times you practise mirroring, it might seem contrived or parrot-like. Our advice is, nevertheless, to try it with the same enthusiasm as when you want to learn to play a new instrument. In the beginning, the instrument sounds shrill and monotonous, until you master technique and music begins to emerge.

This is also what happens when you begin to use the mirroring process. Most people might need a little practice before they begin to feel the "magic". When your partner, who holds the mirror and reflects your narrative and experiences, suddenly empathizes and understands everything you say and feel, then you almost feel as if you are touched by a magic wand. In a way, it is like having a mirror in front of you so that you can begin to see yourself more clearly and perhaps with new eyes and insights.

Even though it should be a human right, some people never have the experience of the profoundly moving sensation of being heard and seen precisely for the person they are.

The reason why mirroring works so efficiently, as we describe here, is that the listener chooses to be completely present in body and mind. So, the story told is not just heard and repeated, but also listened to, taken in, and mirrored with acknowledgement and complete empathy. So, for both the storyteller and the listener, this creates a feeling of coherence, being understood, and feeling on the same wavelength again. *Right now we understand each other. Right now I dare open up again. Right now . . .*

STEP 2: ACKNOWLEDGEMENT

When the mirroring of the storyteller's problem or experience is complete, the couple moves on to acknowledgement. At this stage, the listener acknowledges what he or she just heard by telling the storyteller that his or her story makes sense. Briefly, acknowledgement is about saying that you, as the listener, understand the storyteller's problem and can put yourself in his or her position, seeing the world through his or her eyes.

A client once described acknowledgement as putting all your own thoughts into a balloon and floating it in the air, becoming completely present to the other person's story. The issue here is not that we should agree with the storyteller's version of reality, because even if the couple tells the same story, there will always be at least (!) two views of the same issue.

We come now to a really exciting phase: a dance where we are increasingly free from the shadows of childhood. Gradually, we become able to see our partner for who he or she really is.

Acknowledging means affirming that your partner's story makes sense to you: *Your story makes sense because . . .* Here, you acknowledge the important points in your partner's story. You take as your point of departure the summary, emphasizing that the storyteller's words make sense to you and that his or her account is coherent and logical. In the event that some aspects do not make sense, you might say: *Please help me to understand . . .* Then you check again that the storyteller feels understood.

You can stay on your partner's side of the bridge and affirm that his or her story makes sense without agreeing with how your partner might think or feel. So, acknowledgement can, for many people, be experienced as the most difficult aspect of the dialogue process. The core focus of acknowledgement is to create a space where different worlds can meet.

STEP 3: EMPATHY

The third and last step in the dialogue process is empathy. Here, the listener is required to put him or herself in his partner's shoes – this time on an emotional level. At this stage, the listener shows his or her empathy by imagining what the storyteller might feel about the experiences he or she described.

As the listener, you try to imagine how the elements of the story must have affected the storyteller. When the storyteller listens to your suggestions, he or she becomes increasingly aware of feelings associated with the story.

As you cannot know precisely what your partner feels, your expressions of empathy can only be a suggestion. However, as a listener, you need to identify some precise feelings that you think could be evoked by this story.

Now you have heard as well as acknowledged your partner, and tried to empathize with the feelings your partner might have experienced in connection with this story. You offer a guess of one or two feelings:

When you feel like that about the things you have told me, then I think you are left with a feeling of . . . As a listener, you guess at the feeling: *It must have been lonely and you must have felt completely misunderstood and incredibly angry – are these some of the feelings you have?*

The underlying meaning is not relevant here, since that would distract you from the feelings.

As the storyteller, you take some of the feelings you recognize and leave the rest. The listener's guesses focus the storyteller's attention on the feelings about the story when the listener asks: *Are there any more feelings?* until the storyteller says: *No.*

IT IS JUST MORE WONDERFUL AND FUN

I have spent much energy on "acquiring a good childhood", learning to trust myself and my feelings. I have also spent quite a lot of money and time seeing a psychologist who has been able to listen and support me in this process.

However, since my husband and I have learned to listen and be at ease with each other through the Acknowledging Dialogue, I have experienced a significant new development. I can now talk to my husband about the things that frustrate me in our daily life. They might be small or large issues. Above all, I have become aware of the importance of focusing on small issues, or issues that I do not yet fully understand myself. It is then that I and my husband use the Acknowledging Dialogue in order to understand what it is that triggers me, for instance, when I am with the children.

This way of communicating brings a greater closeness and understanding between my husband and me. On a personal level, it has meant that I feel much calmer and secure, have greater self-esteem, and feel confident about my decisions. As an extra bonus, I have become very good at saying yes and no, as well as stating my own needs and limits. I attribute this to the way my husband listens and mirrors me, because in this way I get to know myself, my emotions, and my needs better, thereby taking them more seriously.

There is also more peace and harmony in the family. Now, we experience fewer conflicts between us and the children. The greater intimacy and love between me and my husband has made it more wonderful and fun for us to be a family.

Marianne

IT ALL BEGINS WITH APPRECIATION

We do not think about it, but we constantly influence the energy, the space, and the emotional atmosphere in our family and our relationship. Everything we contribute to this shared space, whether we are together or alone, adds something positive or negative to the space. It may sound a little frightening, but, nevertheless, it is something important to be aware of.

For this reason, it might be a good idea to begin the Acknowledging Dialogue by focusing on the space between us so that there is the confidence necessary to relax and begin to listen to each other's stories. Feeling insecure only locks us into our own worlds, and we will spend our energy protecting ourselves and holding on to our own reality instead of opening up to receive new ideas that could enable us to change. Is there anything better at creating a surge of positive energy than telling our partner what we appreciate about him or her? It can be something he or she has said or done recently. It is a truism that we express the good things in life too little. Why wait for our silver wedding anniversary, a fortieth birthday, or the end of our days to say how much we actually appreciate one another? The Acknowledging Dialogue can always begin and end with each partner expressing an appreciation of the other, as it is impossible to be appreciated too much.

THE ACKNOWLEDGING DIALOGUE STEP BY STEP

SETTING THE SCENE

Take two chairs and sit facing each other where you can easily look each other in the eyes. Put your feet flat on the ground and let your hands rest on your thighs. Keep your hands relaxed; when our hands are open we are more in touch with ourselves. Allow yourself to sink into the chair and notice what it is like to be where you are. If it feels right, take hold of each other's hands. It can enhance the dialogue if you are physically in touch with each other. Holding hands becomes ever more natural as you become more familiar with the dialogue process.

EYE CONTACT

Look each other in the eyes. It is important to maintain eye contact until your thoughts calm down, stop racing, and you can become present and receptive to your partner. Allow your eyes to go exploring with "soft baby eyes". Consider that your full presence is a gift to the other person.

THE APPRECIATION

Take some deep breaths. Allow your thoughts gradually to become an appreciation. Even when you are at odds with one another, it is always possible to think of something good to say to your partner. Remember that if we are constantly met with criticism and demands then there is no chance that we will open up. When we create a safe atmosphere for one another by offering an appreciation, then we can let down our guard.

You could, for instance, say:

Thank you for giving me tea in bed this morning . . .
Thank you for being in my life . . .
I am so pleased that you . . .
I appreciate you for your courage to go through the difficult times with me . . .
You mean something very special in my life . . .

CHOICE OF TOPIC

Tell one another about the topics you would like to discuss and then decide who should first be the storyteller and who the listener. The storyteller has a topic he or she would like to discuss. Now it is the storyteller's job to take the listener on a journey exploring this topic.

THE SPACE AND THE BRIDGE

Now you can both quietly move into the space between you. How does the space which will become your shared "carrier wave" feel? Take your time.

Imagine a bridge between your two worlds. It is a small, narrow bridge, where there is only room for one person at a time. Notice where you are on the bridge.

When both of you are ready, the storyteller invites the listener for a dialogue. Take your time.

The storyteller: *I would like to invite you into my world so that you can hear what I have to say.*

The listener now imagines that he or she crosses the bridge and walks into the partner's world. This means leaving his or her own world and baggage behind, bringing only passport and visa in order to be able to visit his or her partner's world with sincere curiosity and enthusiasm. Only in this way will it be possible to get to know the partner's world, language, and culture.

MIRRORING

By drawing breath deep into the stomach, you create interior space. Keep up the deep breathing, relaxing body and mind to be ready for mirroring.

The Storyteller

Step by step you can now bring to life the frustration or the topic you have chosen to talk about: *The issue that preoccupies me is that . . .*

You begin by describing your frustration or your topic. What is it about, when does it occur, and in what connection, what feelings are associated with this topic, what behaviour follows? It is important not to censure yourself and to share whatever feelings emerge. Remember, you are at the beginning of your story, so it is important that you share whatever comes up. You will find your own rhythm, so the sentences will become precise and not too long. The listener can then mirror you as verbatim as possible.

The Listener

You begin by mirroring and you need to ensure that you always mirror everything the storyteller says precisely. When you mirror your partner's language precisely, you will become sensitive to his or her words and choices of words. The effect of this is that you will gradually and subtly be transported into your partner's world. Take your time to look at your partner before you start mirroring. Gaze at your partner. Read in your partner's face what your attentiveness means to him or her and end every mirroring with the words: *Was that what you said? Did I get everything?*

Then you can continue with the words: *Tell me more,* or *Is there more you want to say?*

If you cannot remember what you are supposed to mirror, you just say: *Please tell me that again.*

If you happen to run back "home" across the bridge, then remember to tell your partner. You could, for instance, say: *Now I have run "home" again . . . and now I am coming back to you.*

SUMMARY

The Listener
Gives a short summary of what the storyteller has shared. The listener then concludes with the words:

Did I get the essential issues? or *Was it an OK summary?*

The Storyteller
Confirms or disconfirms that the essential issues were in the summary. If he or she wishes, the storyteller can add something to the summary, which the listener then mirrors.

ACKNOWLEDGEMENT

The Listener
During the acknowledgement, the listener maintain a curious attitude, "tastes" the storyteller's narrative, and experiences without making any judgements as to whether they are right or wrong. The listener conveys that he or she has understood the storyteller's story. The listener attempts to see the world through the eyes of the storyteller without needing to be in agreement with the storyteller about the interpretation.

The listener could, for instance, begin the acknowledgement by saying:

It makes sense to me that . . .

I understand that you have experienced things the way you just told me.

What I understand, when I see things from your point of view is that . . .

If there is something the listener has not understood, he or she could say:

Help me to understand by elaborating on the issue concerning . . .

The listener then summarizes the main points of what the storyteller just said, ending with the words: *Do you feel that I have understood you?*

The Storyteller
Yes, I feel understood, or you have understood quite a lot, or I would also like you to understand that . . .

The Listener
Mirrors and acknowledges the storyteller.

EMPATHY

The Listener
Could, for instance, say:

I imagine that this has made you feel . . . (use only two or three words that best describe the feeling).

The Storyteller
Confirms and repeats the emotions which describe the experience.

The Listener
Asks: *Are there any other feelings?*

If there are more feelings, then he or she mirrors these.

CONCLUSION

Sharing
Remaining seated, notice what the shared space between you now feels like. Remember to maintain eye contact and keep your hands open. What feelings do you sense characterize the emotional space between you now? Notice what you are thinking and say it out loud.

Concluding Appreciation
The dialogue can end with a mutual appreciation of the way in which the other person has contributed to the process.

When you want to switch roles, the listener can become the storyteller and vice versa, so the dialogue on the same topic may continue or you can introduce a new topic.

OUR NEW BABYSITTER

We have three sons of three, five, and eight years. After dinner, they often play on the floor with Lego. One of the major challenges facing my husband and me is how to plan our days. Often, we end up fighting and create a bad atmosphere. One evening we were again about to start such a fight. We were sitting in the kitchen with a cup of coffee while the children were playing with Lego on the floor. The minute we raised our voices, the eldest boy of eight came to us, trying to get our attention.

The moment I saw his worried young gaze, it struck me that we had to take responsibility for the bad atmosphere. We were able to do so this because we had just attended a seminar about the "Acknowledging Dialogue". At the seminar we had practised taking turns storytelling and listening, and also visiting each other's worlds. I smiled at my husband and asked him if he felt like trying a dialogue.

The moment we began talking together in the acknowledging way, we experienced that our son was back in the game playing with his brothers and the Lego. He was again able to lose himself in the game and we could concentrate on our tasks.

Malene

THE MIRACLE OF ACKNOWLEDGEMENT

There are many reasons that the Acknowledging Dialogue has such a strong and liberating effect on the people who use it. The slow pace and silence that occurs when we mirror each other without reacting to the storyteller's thoughts and feelings helps the insights form almost as strings of pearls, as old memories are given time and space to surface and become accessible. Silence is golden when it is allowed to exist without being forced. In situations like this, surprising new memories, feelings, and thoughts emerge. When you are in a personal flow and in a close and safe situation with your partner, who is sitting in front of you with attentive, curious, and engaged eyes and ears, then there is a real opportunity to enter new territory and become wiser together.

On a physical level, the calm and the silence also have the effect that you feel your body in a way you rarely experience it on a day-to-day basis. You have the opportunity to "feel" your thoughts and their presence in your body, enabling you to access childhood memories, which you would otherwise not be able to voice and visualize.

Physical sensations might be pressure in the chest, a stone in the stomach, or a diffuse sense of unease. When we attempt to connect these sensations with experiences from childhood or later life, this detective work can help us to access and understand the stories that accompany the feelings of sadness, anxiety, and frustration. Using this approach, it becomes possible to access the longings which are always behind any frustration. By expressing the longings, we can restore the safe, essential connection, and this will become an important experience for the couple.

At first it may seem that your partner is the reason for your frustration. But now – kazaam! – he or she is also the person who will be your safe and intimate helper. At first, it might only be possible when using the clear structure of the Acknowledging Dialogue. However, you will gradually realize that your sense of safety will spread like ripples on water and become a more permanent aspect of the space between you.

The miracle is that you, as a listener, do not have to provide solutions or generate results for your partner. All you have to do is to listen and acknowledge what you hear. By creating this acknowledging dialogical space, you are doing the best you can as a partner and parent to resolve conflicts and frustrations and allow new options to emerge spontaneously.

CAN WE REALLY DO THIS?

Perhaps you ask yourself if you can really do all this, if you can remember it and, not least, dare to see it through! Anyone who has the will and the courage to be sincere and open can make progress. Consider the fact that we have all, at one time or another, been confident with this intimate dialogue and shared a large amount of freedom and confidence with our partner. Otherwise, we would never have got together in the first place. That intimacy can be retrieved. You might be the one to take the initiative in trying to restore intimacy with your partner. At first, it might seem awkward and contrived to work within a structure that prescribes how to talk about such difficult and sensitive issues. However, you will find that it is precisely this structure, with the mirroring, which enables something different to happen. The structure of the dialogue will help you and your partner experience again the indescribable joy of being heard in the way you long for. You may also find that you have a new way to work on issues that create problems for you, so that new understandings and new behaviours can emerge.

If you and your partner find this work difficult to do on your own, you can always continue the work with a therapist who is trained to use these dialogical tools. The therapist can teach you ways to integrate the Acknowledging Dialogue into your daily lives.

AN EXAMPLE OF THE ACKNOWLEDGING DIALOGUE

THE SETUP

Anders and Dorthe have been married for eleven years. The family consists of Anders and Dorthe, Dorthe's two sons from a previous marriage, Frederik, aged seventeen, and Tobias, aged thirteen, and Anders and Dorte's daughter, Amalie, aged three. For some years, Anders and Dorthe have worked with the Acknowledging Dialogue. They face each other and move about on their chairs until they have found a comfortable position. Dorthe's knees are between Anders' knees, upon which his open hands are at rest. They seek eye contact, smile a little, look down, and try again. It is quiet, and the point of this setup is to create a safe space with maximum attentiveness.

INITIAL APPRECIATION

Dorthe: I would like to invite you to my place in order to tell you something that I appreciate about you. I appreciate you because you are so sincere and try to be open in your relationship with me – even if it is sometimes difficult.

Anders: You would like to appreciate that I am sincere and open towards you – even if it is difficult. Was that what you said?

Dorthe: Yes. I also want to appreciate your concrete way of showing it. Even if you are hurt, you stay "on my side" and remain open and attentive.

Anders: You appreciate my sincerity and that I, even if I am hurt, try to remain open towards you.

Dorthe: Yes, I feel valued when you approach me in that way.

Anders: You feel valued when I meet you with an open attitude.

Dorthe: Yes, that gives me a feeling of . . . (Dorthe reflects) happiness and gratitude.

Anders: It makes you happy and grateful . . . Is there more?

Dorthe: (She reflects again) . . . No, that is fine.

Anders appreciates Dorthe

Anders: The feeling that surfaces right now is that I appreciate you when I experience you as independent and responsible.

Dorthe: What you appreciate in me right now is independence – when I am independent and take responsibility. Is that correct?

Anders: Yes, I appreciate many things about you. What I have appreciated recently is that you hold on to your opinions and feel OK when your opinions differ from mine – when you dare to disagree – and the difference does not make you feel insecure.

Dorthe: What I hear you say is that you like to see that, for instance, when we disagree, I remain true to my opinions. Was that what you said?

Anders: Yes, that was what I meant. When I experience you in that way, I feel confident. I feel equal and close to you.

Dorthe: It gives you a feeling that we are equals.

Anders: Yes, as well as a feeling of connection.

Dorthe: And a feeling of connection . . . Is there more?

Anders: No, that was all.

CHOICE OF A TOPIC

Anders: I have an issue that we might explore together – something that could be good to discuss, which could help both of us. Would that be OK?

Dorthe: That is fine.

Anders: Are you ready to come to my place and listen to my story?

Dorthe: Yes.

Anders: I would like to talk about how we have behaved as parents in relation to our eldest son. On a concrete level, this topic arises from a recent episode in which you described me as temperamental to some of our acquaintances

Dorthe: Because I recently described you as temperamental, you would like to talk about the way in which we have behaved as parents to Frederik?

Anders: You are on to something which to me is extremely and profoundly serious. It deserves a much more thorough description than merely being labelled as temperamental.

Dorthe: You feel that this matter is too serious to just be labelled temperamental.

Anders: Yes, because I do not feel that this corresponds to my version of reality.

Dorthe: This does not correspond to the way you see reality.

Anders: No, and for this reason it sparked in me a need to talk about my experiences as a parent to Frederik and how you idealize by glossing over some parts of the story. In my view, you romanticize the story.

Dorthe: You think that my version of the story of our parenting of Frederik is too idyllic.

Anders: In my view, the story is more serious and painful. It is a burden to me, but one I choose to carry.

Dorthe: To you the story is more painful.

Anders: Yes, and for this reason I would like to talk about how we think about the past in relation to Frederik, because this needs to be dealt with.

Dorthe: For this reason you are preoccupied with how we think about the past in relation to Frederik.

Anders: Yes, between the two of us and also in direct relation to him.

Dorthe: Between the two of us as well as in direct relation to Frederik.

Anders: With the insight and maturity I have now, I find it difficult to look back, especially on how I treated Frederik when he was a child. That was not OK.

Dorthe: It is difficult and tough to think about how we, and especially you, treated Frederik when he was a child.

Anders: Yes, and that was just not OK.

Dorthe: That was just not OK.

Anders: I feel guilt in relation to this issue. It is extremely difficult for me to deal with.

Dorthe: You feel guilty in relation to this issue. And that is tough.

Anders: But I also feel that you share some of the guilt . . . because you did not intervene.

Dorthe: But I might also be guilty, because I did not intervene.

Anders: I have no problems looking back in life and forgiving myself on the basis of my youth and inexperience. Well . . . I was very young. I have no problem forgiving and excusing myself. However, that does not change the fact that it was not OK. For my own sake, but also for Frederik's sake, I feel that what I did should not be called temperamental – this is where I feel provoked. It should just not be labelled like that. It is too serious a matter.

Dorthe: You are saying that it is difficult for you to hear me label your actions as temperamental. It is too serious a matter to just call it temperamental. It should not just have a label. Was that what you said?

Anders: Yes, that is the reason why it is necessary that we talk about it and that I should talk with him about it. But it takes a lot of courage and strength to talk to Frederik about it, because the pain becomes so big and intense.

Dorthe: You need for us to talk to him about it and you should talk to him about it. Was that what you said?

Anders: I feel that you and I need to talk about what happened. What was it like? I feel that we should talk about it separately.

Dorthe: I see, you feel that the two of us should talk about what really happened.

Anders: Yes, and the other thing is that I need to talk to Frederik. I have talked to him a few times and I feel that it is extremely demanding. It is emotionally very challenging for me.

Dorthe: You have already talked to Frederik about it, but you feel that it is very difficult and emotionally demanding. But you feel that you owe it to him.

Anders: Yes, It is something I really want to do. I would also like to do more. I feel that it helps him. It eases his pain when I take responsibility for my actions.

Dorthe: You would like to do it and you feel that it would help him.

Anders: The most difficult thing to think about . . . I have an inner film where he is scolded – no matter what he does, it is wrong. The only thing he can do is to hide . . . by not looking anywhere with open eyes is one way of putting it.

Dorthe: (In a compassionate voice) Part of the problem was that Frederik was scolded no matter what he did. Finally, he shut down and looked with unseeing eyes.

Anders: (In a heavy and low voice) His situation was quite impossible.

Dorthe: He must have been in an impossible situation – and that gives you a bad conscience.

Anders: Yes (very heavy – followed by a long pause) . . . I feel . . . that I am partly responsible for damaging him.

Dorthe: You feel that you are partly responsible for damaging him.

Anders: Yes, and it is so painful that I have treated him in a way that I would never have done if I had had the maturity I have now. I can find all kinds of excuses, but, regardless of the excuses, I cannot bear having treated a child as badly as, in fact, I did. I did not do it all the time . . . I have also treated him well. However, there have been episodes that were not OK. There was scolding and the way it was done was not appropriate . . . (pause). Nowadays, I feel that he was treated so badly that it must have been unbearable for him.

Dorthe: You are saying that you feel that you have treated him so badly that it must have been unbearable for him . . .

Anders: Yes, it is difficult to formulate . . . It is difficult to own up to something which . . . it is almost as if another person did it. It is very difficult to own up to behaving in a way that I understand today is entirely inappropriate. This is part of the reason why it is so difficult for me to talk about it today.

Dorthe: It is difficult to talk about it because you feel that it is something that someone else did because you would not treat him like that today.

Anders: I feel that he became a scapegoat in our lives. Because he was like he was and our immaturity did not help.

Dorthe: You feel that he became a scapegoat because he was the person he was.

Anders: He was a challenge because he was noisy and wild. Full on. He was cute. There was nothing bad about him. But I hurt him a lot.

Dorthe: The difficult thing was that Frederik was uncontrollable and noisy.

Anders: I remember far too many episodes where he was scolded a lot and where the scolding led to dead end situations. It was almost a regular event, going on for a number of years. There was nobody questioning it. He was just scolded a lot.

Dorthe: You remember that there were far too many times when he was scolded a lot and that it went on for a number of years.

Anders: It must have started when . . . it is really difficult to think about . . . from when he was five. It was on the increase, and it became sort of a role for him.

Dorthe: It began at the age of five. It became a role for him.

Anders: In the beginning, he was just scolded a lot. But finally it was as if he was scolded because he was Frederik. If anything happened, he got the blame.

Dorthe: Every time there were problems, Frederik was blamed.

Anders: It is really difficult to talk about . . . It reminds me that he overreacted by feeling guilty about all kinds of things for no reason at all . . . Oh my God . . . He could not figure out if he had done something terrible . . . He was around 12–14 years old. I think he had been scolded so much that he no longer knew what was right and what was wrong. Sometimes, when he had done something really banal, he would come home and ask if what he had done was terribly wrong.

Dorthe: It also hurts to think about how, when Frederik was 12–14 years old, he would come home and not be quite sure if he had done something serious even if it was completely banal. He had problems distinguishing between right and wrong.

Anders: It was also physical . . . I pulled him. I shook him. I grabbed him. It was not only on a verbal level.

Dorthe: You remember that you shook him and grabbed him.

Anders: I also hit him.

Dorthe: You also hit him.

Anders: I remember that he was around eight or nine years old. I was so furious that I threw a dishcloth at him. He ducked – he was really good at physical games – so that Tobias got the cloth right in the face and began to cry. I do not know if I remember correctly, but I believe that I hit him. I did lash out at him with the back of my hand. It is difficult for me to remember. But I think that it is correct that I hit him because my memory goes completely blank . . . yes, I hit him.

Dorthe: There was once an episode where you threw a cloth at him, but he ducked. Then you hit him with the back of your hand because the cloth hit Tobias instead and Tobias began to cry.

Anders: I feel it is difficult to face up to. But I must. Not in order to torture myself, but in order to let go of something, also for Frederik's sake.

Dorthe: You feel that you have to deal with it. Not in order to torture yourself, but because you feel that it will be liberating – and also for Frederik's sake.

Anders: I do not mean to blame myself. I have lots of guilt, but I have no problem understanding what happened. I was young and frustrated. We had three children and no money. This was a much greater task than I was prepared for. Emotionally, I was not big enough to be the father of three children. There were also lots of good episodes, but I do not believe in constantly telling the good story while the other story remains untold. It is as if it is too painful for all of us.

Dorthe: You feel that the story about you and Frederik is too painful, that we only talk about all the good things, and that the three of us do not want to remember this story.

Anders: I get a splitting headache talking about it.

Dorthe: You get a splitting headache talking about it.

Anders: But I also feel that it is right and important. These days, Frederik says that he is so fond of me. He loves it when I give him special attention. And I become incredibly happy when he tells me this, while at the same time also feeling that . . . (hesitates) it is very wonderful . . . But all the other things must also be said.

Dorthe: You say that Frederik says that he loves you and is happy that you care for him. But this is almost too much for you.

Anders: I would really like you to understand that I am very interested in discussing this matter thoroughly with you and that we should dare to do it. We should talk about it and talk to Frederik about it. I think he needs that. It is a shadow in his life. It is also important for to me to say that I found that Frederik provoked me. He has always done what I dared not to do. I have always tried to be considerate and please other people . . . He would always take the largest piece of cake.

Dorthe: You feel it is important that we talk this over in detail, and that we talk to Frederik about it. You also feel that you find something about Frederik provokes you. For instance, the fact that he did the opposite to you – where you have been considerate, Frederik has been quite the reverse, thinking only of himself.

Anders: It is also important that you understand that it is a matter between the two of us. I feel that you also need to clarify this issue and your part in it.

Dorthe: You think it is a matter between the two of us, and that I also need to understand my part in this conflict.

Anders: Yes, that you have also been part of this process. We need to shed some tears. We need to apologize. I think this would be good for us. It would mean a greater honesty in our relationship.

Dorthe: You think we need to face up to this and apologize. And you believe it can bring more honesty into our relationship.

Anders: Yes, I think that when a story enters our lives, for instance the story about my temper, then we do not live full lives. I need to dare to go all the way and own up to what happened so that we can live truthful lives. My intention is not to experience a lot of pain, but to be more . . . liberated. Both of us in our way can . . .

Dorthe: (Feels sad and does not listen) I did not quite hear what you just said . . .

Anders: I think we both in our way can get a little too . . . comfortable.

Dorthe: You feel that you and I can become a little too comfortable (in a weak voice, she is touched).

Anders: Yes, this is not a wonderful story. On the other hand it is a true story . . .

Dorthe: It is not a wonderful story, but it is a true story.

Anders: What I mean is that if I had agreed with you that I am temperamental, then we would have constructed a story that was pleasant and comfortable to live with, but that story would not have been true.

Dorthe: If you had agreed with me about being temperamental then you would have experienced us telling a story that was untrue.

Anders: I think that if we stick to that story, then we will continually be doing Frederik a wrong. I think that if we talk about it as best we can, then we can contribute to the healing of his wounds.

Dorthe: If we talk about it as best we can, then we contribute to the healing of Frederik's wounds.

Anders: Yes, and in terms of our relationship, I think it would become more authentic and truthful.

Dorthe: You think our relationship will become more authentic and true, if we talk about it.

Anders: Yes, because I feel a kind of protest against turning it into an idyll.

Dorthe: You feel a protest against our romanticizing the story.

Anders: Yes, I think that it could be a great help if the two of us began to talk about what actually happened. It would help if we could feel sad together and help each other out. We both did what we could, but still things were not OK.

Dorthe: It would help you if the two of us sat down and talked about what happened then.

Anders: Yes, we should embrace the challenge with the more mature attitude we have today. I would like you to help me embrace my guilt by listening to me and helping me dare to feel it. And I could help you do the reverse. Then we could work this problem through thoroughly, and the next step would be to include Frederik.

Dorthe: You believe that we can help each other, because we are more mature today and that we can subsequently help Frederik.

Anders: It would be a great release for me and it would relieve me of a great responsibility. But it would also mean a greater respect between us.

Dorthe: You would feel relieved by taking on this responsibility. It would also mean a greater respect between us.

Anders: In relation to Frederik, it would mean that both of us would have an easier time talking about it. That would be healthy for him as well as for me.

Dorthe: Talking about it and helping each other would mean that it would be easier for you to talk to Frederik about it. That would be good for both of you.

Anders: In terms of our relationship, I would feel more love and what I said in the appreciation – a greater feeling that we are honest, brave, and adult.

Dorthe: It would result in greater maturity and honesty between us.

Anders: Yes, and our relationship would become even stronger and more liberated.

Dorthe: You imagine that our relationship would become even stronger and more liberated.

Anders: I feel compelled to live a more authentic life, as true a life as possible.

Dorthe: You also feel a great desire to live as authentically as possible.

Anders: The link to my own story, my baggage, is that I grew up with idyllic stories, but a reality that was diametrically opposed and different. In my family we were – on the surface – very loving towards each other and would always be there for one another.

But in reality, I lived almost alone from when I was twelve years old. I do not want to live with that contradiction.

Dorthe: You are saying that in your family you were very loving and would always be there for each other. But in reality, you were on your own – nobody was there for you. This is the idyllic story and the contradiction you can no longer live with.

Anders: So, when in our family there is just an inkling of not wanting to call a spade a spade, then that "short-circuits" something in my story.

Dorthe: So, when our family experiences just a trace of not wanting to call a spade a spade, then that blocks something in your life.

Anders: Yes, in my story there is a great longing to be able to be completely honest in a relationship and with myself.

Dorthe: You have a great longing to be able to be completely honest in our relationship and with yourself.

Anders: Yes, and I need your support in the process of daring to tear all the walls down.

Dorthe: And in this process you need my support in tearing all the walls down.

Anders: I imagine that this could be rather challenging to you.

Dorthe: You also imagine that this could be a challenge to me.

Anders: Yes, because you are very authentic and truthful. On the other hand, there might be places where you do not want to go. I would like to go there. I would like to go there and connect with that level.

Dorthe: You see me as very authentic and truthful. On the other hand, you feel that there are places I do not want to go. You would like to go to those places and connect with those levels.

Anders: In relation to Frederik, I believe that in this way we can help him to go to the places where he has difficulties. His impulse is still to withdraw. He is good at expressing love, but not difficult emotions. He does not tell us, but we can feel them. He tells us how much he loves us, but he does not tell us how difficult we can be for him. In this way, we could perhaps heal some of the wounds we inflicted on him.

Dorthe: You think that Frederik is good at expressing love, but you also see that he has difficulties in relation to us, even if he does not say so. In this way, you think that we can heal some of the wounds we have given him.

Anders: Yes, and the reason why I think this is that he still lives with the fear he experienced in his childhood. Even if we have changed, he is still stuck there. Because it is so full of conflict he does not share it with us.

Dorthe: You think that Frederik still lives in the fear he experienced in his childhood. You also think that he does not share it with us because it is full of conflict.

SUMMARY

Dorthe: You would like to discuss an episode where we talked about Frederik and I mentioned your temper. You reacted to this by saying that you did not want a serious issue merely to be labelled temperamental, since it is not only a question of temperament. It is much more serious, and you would like to discuss it thoroughly with me. You would like to talk to me about your, mine, and Frederik's story. Your focus is that something went wrong between the two of you. The problem was that Frederik was scolded too much and that that was very difficult for him. You remember many episodes which you find it difficult to think about and talk about, but we have to do this because we owe it to Frederik. We have moved on in our lives, but it means a lot to you to give Frederik an opportunity to heal the wounds he got when he grew up with the two of us.

You have talked to Frederik about it, and you were both deeply affected by the conversation. You feel very guilty and have a bad conscience, but you also think that I need to take some of the responsibility. You feel that I should have intervened and stopped it. You realize that all this has something to do with our respective backgrounds and youth, that it was difficult to become parents at such an early age. You were twenty when you became the father of two young boys. In the light of your youth and our immaturity at the time, we treated Frederik in a way which we find difficult to own up to today, but we have to deal with it. Did I get the most important issues?

Anders: Yes, you got the most important things. Frederik's character, the way he was at odds with the way in which I grew up. He was everything I was not. He did all the things I had been taught not to do. I believe that if you and I could talk about it in the light of our present maturity, then we could better get to grips with what happened back then. It might be beneficial to us and to Frederik in terms of more honesty, which is important to me.

Dorthe: The reason was that Frederik was so different from you. He did the things you had been taught not to do. If the two of us can talk about that, given our present maturity, it would also help Frederik. It could also mean that we would become more honest with each other.

Anders: Yes, because I am allergic to idyllic versions of reality. I long for the opposite.

Dorthe: You are allergic to idyllic stories and long for the opposite.

ACKNOWLEDGEMENT

Dorthe: It makes sense when you say that your relationship with Frederik is too serious and painful to be labelled as temperamental. It makes sense that you experience that we – and you in particular – have hurt Frederik, but that I also am responsible for not intervening and stopping it. It also makes sense that you were an immature father and that it is painful to look back at the way in which we treated Frederik, given the maturity and the insight we have today. Furthermore, it makes good sense when you say that there have been many episodes where he was scolded a lot and that he could not get out of those situations. He just had to close off and look away with unseeing eyes. In addition, it makes sense that you should be allergic to idyllic stories of reality. The reason is that you actually had to look after yourself from the age of twelve, even if everything in your family looked picture-perfect on the surface and as if you were always there for each other. Hence, it makes sense that we, in our family, do not talk about the way we actually treated Frederik. Moreover, it makes sense that we should work through this together – that we should talk about it – and then share it with Frederik. Do you experience that I have understood you?

Anders: Yes. What I would really like you to understand is that the way in which we treated Frederik was truly out of line. And, by the way, this discussion has nothing to do with me reconciling myself with my past, before Frederik is fully adult. This is serious business.

Dorthe: You would like me to understand that you are serious about this issue and that it is not a selfish endeavour so many years after the fact.

Anders: Yes, and it is important to me that you understand that I sometimes experience that you inadvertently disregard the gravity of this issue. I have not used these terms before, but it is important that you understand that with such avoidances we do not get to the heart of the matter. We just forget the story.

Dorthe: You experience that I sometimes silence the story.

Anders: Yes, and I believe you do that because it is painful for you.

Dorthe: You think that I sometimes silence the story because it is too painful for me.

EMPATHY

Dorthe: Having told me your story, I imagine that you are left with feelings of . . . despair, shame, and hope.

Anders: There is grief . . . and maybe despair. There is something vulnerable and soft, but on the edge of that there is also some anger and frustration.

Dorthe: You experience grief and something vulnerable and soft. However, there is also something bordering on anger – a frustration.

Anders: Moreover, I feel a great compassion towards the way I imagine Frederik must have felt. I also feel compassion towards us – a sense that there is hard work ahead.

Dorthe: You feel compassionate towards Frederik and the things he went through. But you also feel compassionate towards us because of how hard it was for us. Are there any other emotions?

Anders: Yes, you said hope. I feel a hope that is related to you and Frederik – a hope that something good will come of this.

Dorthe: You also feel a hope that something good will come out of all this, that you, me, and Frederik will somehow benefit.

CONCLUDING APPRECIATION

Anders: I appreciate the fact that you made an effort to stay "on my side of the bridge" to listen and understand my story.

Dorthe: You appreciate that I made an effort to remain in your place and tried to understand what it is like to be you.

Anders: I also appreciate the tears that came to your eyes, when I talked about the pain.

Dorthe: You also appreciate the tears that came into my eyes when you talked about the pain.

Anders: Yes, I felt that you understood the pain I feel that Frederik experienced.

Dorthe: You experience that I understood the pain that you feel Frederik must have gone through.

Anders: Your tears give me a feeling of security and connection. Then I can bear all the pain.

Dorthe: It gives you a feeling of security and connection when you see that your story touches me.

THE DIALOGUE IS REVERSED AND DORTHE APPRECIATES:

Dorthe: Anders, I appreciate your profound honesty and the fact that you own up to what you have experienced.

Anders: You appreciate my profound honesty and the fact that I own up to my experience.

THE ACKNOWLEDGING DIALOGUE
FOR PARENTS

In order to get a handle on all the respective conflicts between children and parents, we have developed a special variation of the Acknowledging Dialogue between parents who focus on:

- what our frustrations as parents remind us of;
- a shared reflection on our behaviour and the feelings we have as parents;
- wishes for change.

The purpose is to develop our self-understanding and understanding of each other as parents and, thereby, create a space in which our children can develop. Ultimately, we want to see our children with new eyes and with a calm, open mind. When we do that, we can effectively avoid making the same mistakes as our parents. We can also stop ourselves from passing on bad behaviour patterns to our children.

Like the Acknowledging Dialogue, the dialogue for parents is based on acknowledging and mirroring. However, the Acknowledging Dialogue is expanded to include childhood memories, events in our childhood that our frustrations remind us of. There is always an emotional bridge to childhood memories or other memories connected to significant relationships, be it an inattentive mother, an ex-lover, or a frightening German teacher. We can all leave these emotional links behind and discover the origin of our congruent frustrations, criticism, dissatisfaction, or anger. This process is embedded in the beliefs about communicating in acknowledging ways, as in the Acknowledging Dialogue.

Moreover, the Acknowledging Dialogue for Parents involves four requests for change:

- two requests involving the couple: the storyteller asks the listener to choose one of two options to change some aspect of their behaviour towards the storyteller;
- two requests involving the couple and a child: the storyteller asks the listener to choose one of two options to change some aspects of his or her behaviour with a child.

First of all, the concrete wishes give the couple an opportunity to discover something that they can open up and work on until they find closure. Second, it is an exercise in the formulation of what each desires and would like to have more of, rather than continuing to focus on the things they do not want. Only when longings become concrete requests and are shown in tangible actions do parents have a real opportunity to begin to practise new patterns of action for the benefit of their children.

The aim of the Acknowledging Dialogue for Parents is to facilitate the couple in the making of specific, measurable requests for behaviour change in one another.

THE ACKNOWLEDGING DIALOGUE FOR PARENTS

THE SETUP
Take a seat on two chairs facing each other. The distance between your faces should be approximately 50 cm. Keep your hands open. Sink into the chair and feel what it is like to be where you are.

EYE CONTACT
Look each other in the eyes. It is important to maintain eye contact until the thoughts begin to settle and lose momentum, so that you can be present and receptive.

THE APPRECIATION
An appreciation could, for instance, sound like:

What I appreciate about you as a parent is that . . .

And that you show it by . . .

I really appreciate that you as a parent actually . . .

To me this means that . . .

And that leaves me with the feeling that . . .

CHOICE OF A TOPIC

In relation to a child, a frustration might be:

- something your partner does in his or her relationship with your child;
- a frustration I have in relation to our child.

THE SPACE AND THE BRIDGE

You can now gradually move into the space between you. How does the space feel? From now on, it will be the "carrier wave" between the two of you. Imagine the bridge between your two worlds. It is a small, narrow bridge, where there is room for only one person at a time.

When one of you is ready, he or she (the storyteller) invites his or her partner (the listener) to a dialogue.

The storyteller: I would like to invite you into my world so that you can hear what I have to say.

The listener now imagines that he or she moves across the bridge and into the partner's world.

MIRRORING

The storyteller begins to describe how the selected topic affects the relationship in the here and now.

- your frustrating behaviour (I become frustrated when you scold our child too vehemently);
- my feeling (then I become sad and frightened);
- my response (I become silent);
- what I fear (that we will become distant and that our child begins to feel insecure and sad).

The listener reflects what is said. Did I get everything? Is there more?

Remember to continue the deep breathing. It relaxes the body and the mind. By drawing your breath all the way to the bottom of your lungs, you create interior space.

SUMMARY

The listener gives a summary of the storyteller's story.

Is this an OK summary . . .?

THE ACKNOWLEDGEMENT

The listener expresses the view that the story he or she has heard makes sense and sees the narrative through his or her eyes.

I can understand what you say and it makes sense that you should feel and think the way that you do . . . Do you feel that I have understood you?

EMPATHY

The listener suggests what feelings might be involved for the storyteller.

I can imagine that your feelings in this situation might be that . . . Are these the feelings you have, and are there any others?

CHILDHOOD MEMORIES – THIS REMINDS ME OF . . .

For some people, it can feel difficult and awkward to share disconnected and apparently scattered memories. However, it is important to be open to any memory that surfaces, whether it is a good or a bad recollection. There is no need to try to connect it to a present frustration, because as the story unfolds, the connection will become clear. Allow the process time – sit with the sentence *This reminds me of . . .* until something emerges. It becomes easier every time you try.

1. The storyteller shares how the present feelings remind him or her of earlier experiences:
   I felt that . . . What I really longed for was . . . The way it should have been was that . . .
   The listener mirrors.

2. The listener summarizes in the form of a story:
   There was once a little girl/little boy who . . .

3. The listener puts him or herself into the story:
   If I could enter the story, I would tell your parents that . . . I would tell your mother/father that . . .

There is something I want to tell you which concerns your son/daughter . . .

4. The listener connects the storyteller's childhood memory with the present frustration:
    So now it makes complete sense to me that when I . . . then it makes you feel . . .

5. The listener guesses at the feelings that are intrinsic to the story.

The storyteller acknowledges some feelings and can add other feelings. The listener mirrors.

WHAT I LONG TO RECEIVE FROM YOU . . .

The storyteller identifies two positive quantifiable and specific requests in relation to the frustration. Being able to make a positive request is an important part of the process. We naturally find it easier to say what we do not want rather than what we want.

When we express a longing as a concrete request for action, then we need to ask for something positive, quantifiable, and specific. What we mean by that is something you want your partner to do, and not something you want your partner to stop doing. That would be interpreted as a criticism and would disempower your partner. Quantifiable refers to how often and the number of times you want your partner to carry out your request. The detail is important in this scenario. The word specific means that you describe your request in concrete ways so that your partner is in no doubt about what you want: *Every morning in the coming week, I would like you take the time to say goodbye to everybody in the family before going to work.*

Doing this in a new way can be challenging. We call this kind of behaviour a stretch. We believe we should be willing to stretch ourselves into new ways of behaving even if the stretch seems too big a challenge in relation to our partner and our children.

My first request to you as a partner is . . .
The request is mirrored.

My second request to you as a partner is . . .
The request is mirrored.

The listener then makes a choice and commits to one of the requests.

MY REQUEST TO YOU IN RELATION TO OUR CHILD
The storyteller formulates two positive quantifiable and specific wishes that he or she would like the listener to fulfil in relation to their child.

My first request to you as a parent is . . .
The request is mirrored.

My second request to you as a parent is . . .
The request is mirrored.

The listener then makes a choice and commits to one of the requests.

THE DOUBLE GIFT
The storyteller shares what it means to him or her that the listener wants to meet his or her request and how this connects with childhood memories.

The listener shares what it means to him or her to meet the storyteller's request and how this connects with childhood memories and the meaning of stretching into new behaviour. The listener can find the beginnings of a new story here, a story that can lead to new dialogues.

THE APPRECIATION
The storyteller appreciates the listener:

What I appreciate about you is your way of being present during this dialogue . . .
What this means to me is that . . .
And the feeling this gives me is that . . .

The appreciation is mirrored by the listener.

The listener appreciates the storyteller.

The appreciation is mirrored by the storyteller.

AN EXAMPLE OF THE ACKNOWLEDGING DIALOGUE FOR PARENTS

Anders and Dorthe change the subject to their two oldest children, Frederik, aged seventeen, and Tobias, aged thirteen, using a dialogue designed for parents.

THE APPRECIATION

Dorthe: I would like to begin by inviting you to cross the bridge to my world. I would like to appreciate you because what matters most right now is that you just let me be the person I am.

Anders (mirrors): I hear you say that what you appreciate about me and what matters most right now is that I can let you be the person you are. Was that what you said?

Dorthe: Yes, and you show it by letting go of any idea of what is right.

Anders (mirrors): So you experience that I show you that I want you to be the person you are by letting go of the idea of what is right.

Dorthe: On a concrete level, you give me this experience by accepting me and my differences even if in many ways we are very dissimilar, and I appreciate that very much.

Anders: You know how different we are and you experience that I allow you to be different and to be the person you are.

Dorthe: On a concrete level, you, for instance, say to me that you are happy that I get so much joy from looking after my animals.

Anders: On a concrete level, I might, for instance, share my joy at seeing you so contented with your animals . . . was that what you said?

Dorthe: Yes, and to me that means that I can live my life to the full.

Anders: This has the effect on you that you can live your life to the full, that you can be yourself and enjoy life. Was that what you said?

Dorthe: Yes.

Anders: Would you like to come to my place and hear my appreciation? Right now, while we are sitting here, I appreciate your way of being here. I experience you as being fully present and vibrant and that touches me. I appreciate your ability to be like that.

Dorthe: What you appreciate right now is my closeness. It touches you . . . the fact that I am completely present in this moment.

Anders: Yes, It is difficult for me to express what it is that you do that gives me that experience. It has something to do with your voice and the look in your eyes. They give me a sense of complete sincerity and that affects me.

Dorthe: So you are telling me that my voice and the look in my eyes give you a feeling of complete sincerity.

Anders: Yes, I am affected by your voice and your eyes. They make me feel soft, but also naked and vulnerable . . . and grateful.

CHOICE OF TOPIC

Both select a topic which they would like to discuss.

Anders: I am frustrated because you live so much in the present that you never have time to think about what our home looks like, how the inside of our home is arranged.

Dorthe: It frustrates you that I do not have time to arrange the inside of our home.

My topic is that I would like you to be more present in relation to our children. Specifically with regard to Tobias, who asks for your presence. I feel that he misses that.

Anders: Your theme is that you wish that I had a closer relationship with our children, especially Tobias. You feel that he misses that.

Anders and Dorthe agree to discuss Dorthe's frustration.

FRUSTRATION

Dorthe: Sometimes when we are all three sitting in the living-room, you take out your computer and put it in front of you. I sense that Tobias is looking forward to the three of us having a talk. But the computer gets in the way and Tobias sits there looking at you. That frustrates me.

Anders: You feel that Tobias would like the three of us to have good talk and then I bring out my computer and switch it on. Was that what you said?

THE EMOTION

Dorthe: When that happens, I feel sad and powerless.

Anders: When you experience that, you become sad and you also feel powerless.

Dorthe: Then I try to get you to put the computer away and talk to Tobias. When I do that, Tobias says that we should just leave you alone.

Anders: You, for instance, ask me to close the computer so we can talk. Then Tobias says that it is OK and that you should just leave me alone. Was that what you said?

Dorthe: I might also manipulate you to get you to talk to Tobias or to the other children. I hear myself trying to arrange a connection for you.

Anders: You might also try to manipulate me and arrange something that will make us feel closer. Was that what you said?

Dorthe: Yes, and that makes me feel powerless because I cannot help the boys become closer to you.

Anders: So that leaves you with a feeling of powerlessness, since you cannot help them become closer to me. Was that what you said?

Dorthe: Yes, and I would like to add that I know how much the children love you and your closeness when they experience it. They say how important you are to them, and how important it is that we are together.

Anders: Another thing is that you know how much the children love me. When you hear them talking about me they say how important I am to them. You know how significant I am to them and how vital it is for them to experience my closeness. Was that what you said?

Dorthe: No, I did not say that. I said that the children say that it is important that they feel your closeness when we are together. They do not always feel that you are a part of the family simply because you are often not here.

Anders: So what you mean is that they talk about the importance of my presence but that they do not always feel that I am a part of the family, because I am often away.

Dorthe: When I see that happen, I feel very sad deep down inside.

Anders: So you feel sad when you see that happen.

THE REACTION

Dorthe: Then I try to be there for the children as much as possible.

Anders: So when you feel the sadness, you try to be there for the children as much as possible.

Dorthe: I also try to tell them how much you love them.

Anders: Then you tell them how much I love them.

Dorthe: Yes, and then Tobias might say that he does not feel that.

Anders: Then Tobias might say that he does not feel that – when you tell him how much I love him.

Dorthe: Tobias knows how much you work. He says it in such a way that he seems very brave because he knows that it is because you work so much and have so many projects. On the other hand, he does not understand why you want to work so much and why you do not prioritize spending time with him.

Anders: Yes. (Anders stalls a little and then he says): I realize I just "ran home" to my world . . . Now I will cross the bridge again and return to you . . . Tobias says that he cannot feel that I love him, but you also hear him say that he knows that my absence is due to the fact that I work a lot. That is the reason why I am away so much. So you experience him as being brave in relation to my absence. Was that what you said?

Dorthe: Yes, and it is also important for me to say that the frustration concerns your absence, because at home you are very present. That is why the children miss you.

Anders: It is also important for you to mention that there are other situations where they experience that I am here.

Dorthe: Yes, because you are a great gift to us in our family, so I just wanted to make that clear, Anders.

Anders: Yes, you say that I am a great gift to you in your family and, hence, it becomes important to you to say that I am also occasionally very present.

Dorthe interrupts: I said in our family.

Anders: Oops, I went home to my world for a moment there.

Dorthe: Yes, you did.

Anders: I will just try again. You experience that I am a great gift to OUR family and that these emotions and this fear concerns the times when you feel my lack of presence. There are other situations that are different. This became important for you to mention.

THE FEAR

Dorthe: What I fear most in this situation is precisely what you just happened to say when you used the expression "your family". I am so afraid that you will opt out of our family, Anders.

Anders: So what you fear the most is precisely what I just said when I used the expression "your family". What you fear the most is that I leave the family.

Dorthe: Yes, leave our family.

Anders: Yes, leave our family.

Dorthe: And right now I feel that I would not accept that.

Anders: You would not accept that.

Dorthe: No, because I fear that that could mean that I would not experience the same joy sharing time with you and our children, that I would be alone with the children and that you would leave the family. That is my fear.

Anders: So you fear that you will not experience the joy of . . . (Anders searches for the right words) . . . Could you please repeat that? I did not get what you said.

Dorthe: I fear being alone with the children and that you withdraw from the family.

Anders: Your fear is that I withdraw from the family and that you will be alone with the children.

Dorthe: It is not that I am afraid of being alone. In fact, I like that, and I enjoy the children very much – also when you are not there. But I need for us to be a family together. I simply cannot accept that you are absent too often.

Anders: You are not afraid of being alone. You like to be alone now and then and you have no problems being alone with the children. But you also wish to be with me, and you will not accept that I withdraw from the family.

Dorthe: Now something else surfaces. I feel very strongly that the children miss you and that is what hurts me the most.

It makes me sad . . . because this is not just about me, I feel that now. It is about our children and I do not like to see our children feel sad. So when I see Tobias' longing eyes bright with a wish for your attention, then I become incredibly sad.

Anders: What makes you really sad is that you can see in Tobias' eyes that he is yearning for my attention.

Dorthe: Yes, I wish we could avoid the situation where Tobias longs for closeness with you and is then disappointed.

Anders: You would like to avoid the situation where Tobias longs for closeness with me and then doesn't get it.

Dorthe: Yes, because we taught our children that they should ask for what they want and need. When Tobias sits down on the couch and suggests that we have a chat, he is doing precisely that. When he doesn't get what he asks for, I see that he withdraws and gives up.

Anders: You say that we have taught our children to ask for what they need. When Tobias goes ahead and does that, then you see that the light in his eyes goes out when we do not respond adequately. Is there more?

Dorthe: Yes, I talked to Tobias the other day. He said that he can always count on me giving him the time he needs, that I am the human being he feels he resembles the most. He said that I am the person in the family he feels most safe with. Still, he could easily get that safe feeling from you, if you would give it to him. I know you have the ability.

Anders: You had a talk with Tobias and you realized that part of his experience is that you are actually very present, listening to him when he talks to you. And you feel he could also have that experience with me, because you think that I have the ability to be there for him. Was that what you said?

Dorthe: Yes, when you take time off from your work and just say yes, now we should have family time with lots of fun and talk, then you are there for him. I would like to see more of that.

Anders: So when you experience that I ignore my work for the evening and really participate in the family's life, then that makes you very happy. You would like to see more of that. Was that what you said?

Dorthe: I tell myself that our children have a life with their father and that I have to trust that they will work things out with him.

Anders: You say to yourself that it is our life, that I am their father, and that you have to trust that we will work it out together. Is there more?

Dorthe: No. That is what it is all about.

SUMMARY

Anders: You sometimes experience that I am absent in relation to the children. This is especially so with regard to Tobias. We have taught Tobias that he should express his needs, and you see that he takes our advice seriously. Sometimes, you have the experience that Tobias hopes to get a good chat with us, but then I respond poorly and switch on the computer instead. You see how the hope in his eyes is extinguished, how he gives up even if he excuses me because of the fact that I work a lot. But he wonders why I do not just stop working and spend some time with him. All that makes you sad . . . Mainly because you cannot arrange that Tobias becomes closer to me. You realize that all you can do is to hope that we will work it out. I am certainly capable of doing so. You are extremely happy when I ignore my work so that we can spend quality time together. What you fear the most is a situation where I am not there and not part of the family. You are not afraid of being alone, but you would like us to share time with our children. Was that adequate?

Dorthe: Actually, you understood quite a lot of what I said. However, I experience that your summary is too dense and heavy. When I say that you withdraw from the family, I do not mean that you leave us and never return. What I mean is that you are sometimes not quite attentive and present even when we are in the same room. In that way, we do not have the pleasure of knowing you as the person you really are. You do not always offer closeness when it is needed.

Anders: My summary became a little too dense. You are not afraid that I will disappear altogether. You just do not like the fact that I become a ghost in front of the computer, that I am not really present when I am needed. Was that what you said?

Dorthe: Yes, now it is crystal clear.

THE ACKNOWLEDGEMENT

Anders: It makes very good sense that you become sad when you see that Tobias sends out clear signs that he is disappointed because he did not succeed in making contact with me. It also makes very good sense that you would like me to participate when I am needed, and not just disappear into the computer screen. I also understand that you feel powerless, because there is an issue between me and the children that you wish you could change. I appreciate that you are trying to arrange or manipulate us in the direction of greater closeness on my part. Do you feel that I have understood you?

Dorthe hesitates a little, searches for the right words, and then says:

Yes, you say everything there is to say, but I get a little confused when I cannot feel as if you have crossed the bridge all the way to my place, when I am not sure if you really understand how important this is to me.

Anders: You become confused when you cannot quite feel that I have crossed the bridge all the way to your place. Was that what you said?

Dorthe is touched and the tears begin to flow:

There was just something lacking in your eyes, but now it is there. Now you are here. I know you so well and realize that you are capable of being here with your full presence. Thank you for that.

Anders: I also feel it myself, but it is very difficult for me to talk about it while being here at the same time. I am also moved by your tears. The losses you and the children feel make me very sad. I can see that Tobias is trying and that he gives up. Oops, I just ran back to my world. Now I will cross the bridge again and return to you.

Dorthe: I cry because now I really feel that you are here. I have longed for that, also for the children's sake. We do not have time to neglect the family by being absent.

Anders: We do not have time to neglect the family.

Dorthe: No, concerning the absence – *Dorthe smiles through the tears* – our children are such precious human beings and they deserve us to be there for them. I feel that they should also experience what I share with you right now.

Anders: Our children are such precious human beings and we should not take our absences from the family lightly. You also wish that our children should share the closeness you experience with me. Do you feel understood?

Dorthe: Yes!

EMPATHY

Anders: My guess is that you feel very vibrant, but with regard to my absence, you feel sad and alone. I also think that you have a profound feeling of powerlessness. Are there any more emotions?

Dorthe: I have mixed feelings concerning these issues. I feel alive and vibrant because I cry a lot when I sense what all this is about. With regard to your absence, I feel sad and alone, but I also have an intense feeling of powerlessness.

Anders: So you have an intense feeling of powerlessness. Are there any other emotions?

Dorthe: No, I do not think so.

THE CHILDHOOD MEMORY

Dorthe rests a little and dwells on her emotions and thoughts.

Dorthe: I would like to tell you what this reminds me of. It actually reminds me of my mother, who talked a lot but never listened to what I said.

Anders: This reminds you of your mother who, even though she always talked a lot, never listened to what you had to say.

Dorthe: I have lots of memories. My mother had a large turnover of men friends. They lasted no more than a few months at a time. In my memories, my mother and I are mostly alone. I always had to work out most things myself. When I was in first grade, I had been in Denmark for eighteen months, and by then I had learnt Danish. My mother worked all day so my days began at the youth recreation centre at 6.30 a.m. and I stayed there until I was collected at 5.00 p.m. My main experience of childhood has to do with finding out how my mother felt. When I was sad, she often answered: "Do you know how that makes me feel?" Then I was left with a feeling of being completely wrong, while everything was centred on her experience.

Anders: You rewind to the age of seven when you started school and attended the youth recreation centre. You had been in Denmark for eighteen months and you had learnt Danish. You remember how you were taken to the youth recreation centre early in the morning and picked up again at 5.00 p.m. You feel that your childhood was very focused on your mother's emotions. When, for instance, you felt sad, she would say: "Do you realize what the words you just said do to me?" So it all centred on her. Is there more?

Dorthe: Yes, because I was often sad at school. I was very unruly and got into a lot of trouble from my teachers. I was told that I was stupid and was sent out of the classroom. I had to contain all these emotions for the whole day. I did not show my feelings. When I returned home, I cried. When I was happy again, my mother might say: "Well, now you are happy, then I feel left all alone here with my sadness." So I did not quite feel that I was allowed to be either happy or sad.

Anders does not answer right away. He looks at Dorte with great concern and says: I really feel that I am with you now.

Dorthe: I feel that very strongly.

Anders continues the mirroring:

You were scolded a lot in school because you were unruly. You were sad, but you did not show it in school, only when you came home. Then you had a great need to tell your mother about the scolding. When you were happy again, she would occasionally say to you: "Well, you are on top of the world, while I am left with all the sadness." Then it became difficult for you to be either happy or sad. Is there more?

Dorthe: I apologized for that. I would have liked it if she had given me a hug and embraced me. I needed to hear her say that there was nothing wrong with me.

Anders: You said you were sorry for what you said. You wished that she had embraced you and said that it was not your fault, that you were OK.

Dorthe: Just imagine if she had said: "They are not treating you right, but I support you, so you will be able to bear it." I needed to hear that I was OK, or something to that effect.

Anders: You wish that she had supported you and said that you were OK. Is there more?

Dorthe: Yes, there is much more, but I do not think that I should say more just now. If I do, I will just confuse the issue by broaching new subjects.

THE LISTENER SUMMARIZES AS IF TELLING A STORY

Anders: There was once a little girl who had lived in Denmark for eighteen months and who had just learnt to speak Danish. Her mother worked and there were men in her life, but only for a short while at a time. The little girl had the feeling that there was only her and her mother in their little family. When she was a child, the main issue in her life was the state of her mother's emotions – even if she was away from home from early morning until late in the afternoon. The little girl went to a school where she was scolded a lot and where she was told that she was stupid. She carried the pain inside her until she arrived home, where she told her mother about it. However, when she did that, her mother reacted in ways that shifted the focus to herself. She would, for instance, say to the little girl: "Have you any idea what all the things you tell me do to me?", or when the little girl was happy again, the mother would say: "Well, you may be very happy, but I am left alone with my sadness."

This made the little girl feel sorry for her mother and think that she could be neither happy nor sad, because in both cases the mother would be miserable because of her. The little girl apologized, but deep down in her soul she yearned for her mother's embrace, for her mother's voice telling her that she loved her, and that she was sorry to hear about the knocks she had taken during the day. The little girl also hoped that the mother would have supported her in being all right and in being strong enough to cope with the rough treatment.

THE LISTENER ENTERS THE STORY

Anders: If I could travel in time and enter the story with a message for your mother, I would say:

I am not sure that you are aware of this issue and understand what is going on. But when you say to Dorthe that you are left alone with the sadnesss, then you actually add to her pain, because she has been feeling hurt all day and has a deep need for your comfort and help. Do you realize that you make Dorthe feel like a misfit in relation to you? You must stop believing that you are always at the centre of things. You must wake up to the fact that your daughter has carried a heavy weight all day and that now she needs her mother. What you are doing to her is not OK.

THE CONNECTION BETWEEN THEN AND NOW

Anders: When I hear your story it makes good sense that when you see that Tobias wants to share something, then you know from experience how awful it is not to be seen and heard. Because of your own story, you have a special sensitivity to children who want to share something and do not get a positive response. This makes complete sense to me. When you experience that I put my work on hold in order to be fully present, then it also makes a lot of sense that that means so much to you, since that was what your mother should have done. So when you feel that I am absent, you feel sad on your own behalf but also on behalf of Tobias. To me that makes total sense.

THE LONGING

Dorthe: I wish we could always have the closeness we share right now. To me freedom and closeness are two sides of the same coin.

Anders: You wish we could always benefit from the closeness we are sharing right now. To you freedom and closeness are intimately connected.

SPECIFIC REQUESTS

(Please note that in this dialogue there are only two requests, due to the shortage of time.)

The First Request

Dorthe: One request could be that your communication would be completely clear when you are present, as well as when you are not present.

Anders: You request is that I would communicate clearly when I am present, as well as when I am not present.

Dorthe: In relation to the children, I would find it ideal if you could be present when the children are here. Should you feel like doing something else, then you just say: *Right now I would like to do this or that and later I will come back and talk to you again.* Then they know your agenda and where they stand.

Anders: So your request is that when the children are present, then I should be close to them. I should also communicate clearly when I have time to talk and be around and when I have other plans.

Dorthe: Yes, I would like that. The next three times you have a quiet moment with Tobias, I would be very happy if you would give him your full attention or tell him if you need to do something else.

The Second Request

Dorthe: My second request is that three times in the near future you would also give me closeness and nurture. I would be very happy if, when we meet, you would give me your full attention and tell me what is on your mind. You could, for instance, say: *I just want to share some thoughts with you.* You are also welcome to say: *Why don't you make some coffee, then I will tell you what is on my mind.*

Anders: You would like to experience my full attention. One way to do this could be me saying: *Why don't you make some coffee. There is something I would like to share with you.* Is that what you mean?

Dorthe: Yes, the fact is that we would then be together.

Anders: The fact is that we would be together.

Dorthe: . . . And that I make coffee . . . Dorthe laughs disarmingly.

Anders: I would like to meet your request that I should be completely present the next three times I have a quiet moment with Tobias. If I need to do something else, then I will say very clearly: *Now I need to do this and when I return we will continue where we left off.*

Dorthe: I am very pleased about that.

THE DOUBLE GIFT – WHAT IT MEANS TO DORTHE TO RECEIVE THE GIFT

Dorthe: This means that I feel confident. I feel certain that you will take care of it.

Anders: All this makes you feel confident that I will handle the situation. Have I understood you correctly?

Dorthe: Yes, because together we can make a difference. I could not make a difference when I was a child. Back then I could not get the help I am getting now.

Anders: In your present life you can get help, and that means that we can make a difference together.

Dorthe: I imagine that to Tobias this will mean that he experiences that you love him and that he feels loved by you.

Anders: You imagine that this will make Tobias feel loved by me.

Dorthe: Yes, when you give him attention, he will blossom and become happier.

Anders: You imagine that when Tobias experiences this, then he will become very happy and he will begin to develop.

Dorthe: He will feel it and I can hear him say that his father loves him.

Anders: You would like to hear him say: *my father loves me*.

Dorthe: Yes, I would really like that.

Anders: I understand that very well.

Anders and Dorthe pause and linger in each other's gaze. There is a deep tranquillity in their eyes, an inner smile.

WHAT IT MEANS TO ANDERS TO GIVE THE GIFT

Anders: There is a lot of potential in giving this gift for me. To start with, I was very moved by your presence and your appeal to me. I think more of that would do me good. I have a survival strategy in which I do not allow full connection. Having full connection reminds me of my needs. But your story is in itself a gift, which touches me so profoundly that I can override my impulse to be absent.

Dorthe: You feel that there is a lot of potential in this for you. It began with my closeness, which touched, and later my childhood story, which made you feel that it is easier for you to be close to me and Tobias now. Was that what you said?

Anders: I think that was most of what I said; it was certainly what I meant. However, there is something else. You and Tobias appeal to something in me which is undeveloped. For this reason, it is a gift for me to enter this space.

Dorthe: Tobias and I are the type of people who call forth the closeness that you find difficult. That is precisely the reason why my request is a gift to you. Was that what you said?

Anders: Yes, that was precisely what I said.

THE DIALOGUE FOR PARENTS – SHORTER VERSION

A condensed version of the dialogue for parents, which can revitalize the couple relationship and the parenting, might look like:

1. *One thing I long to receive from you is . . .*

2. *The first step I could take, which would make it safer for you to give me what I long for, is . . .*

3. *In order to help me take this first step, you could . . .*

Steps one, two, and three are all mirrored, and then you change the dialogue to give your partner an equal opportunity to say what he or she longs for from you and to discover what you both can do to obtain what you long for.

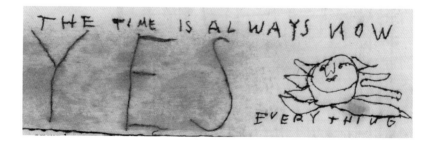

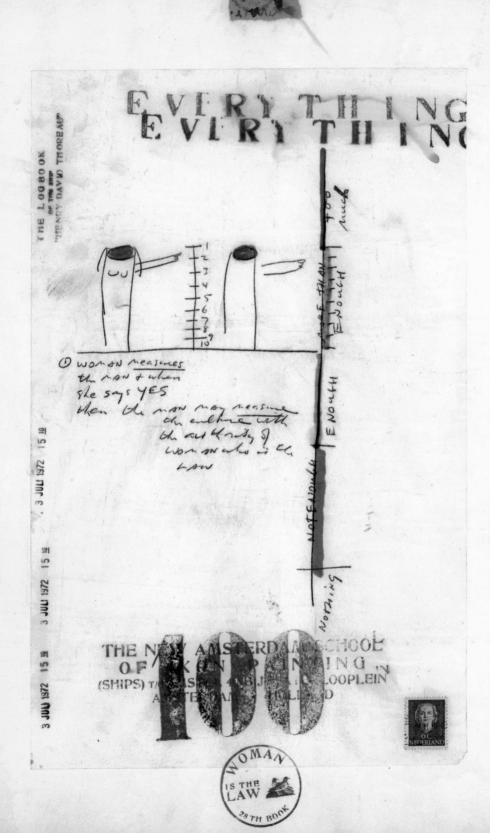

THE ACKNOWLEDGING DIALOGUE
WITH CHILDREN

Developing acknowledging intimacy with our children can be a special challenge because we parents need to be both loving and nurturing, while also taking responsibility for making decisions, choices, and instructing our children at times when they need guidance.

Our job is to point our children in the right direction – even if they might occasionally experience us as unloving. As parents, one hopes we have an overview and the ability to assess the consequences of the choices our children want to make. Yet again, we must say no to eating sweets after they have brushed their teeth, insist on giving them warm clothes when it is cold, and say no to going out for the second night in a row when the homework is piling up.

Perhaps you find it easier to be an attentive parent rather than the parent who has to take responsibility for guiding your child. If this is how you feel, it could be difficult for you to tell your child in no uncertain terms that presently it is bedtime, and that there will be no more evenings out this weekend. You may hope that your child will recognize the importance of such rules. When this does not happen, you probably get annoyed, and might begin to scold and feel like giving up.

If you find it easier to be one kind of parent rather than another, it could be time to explore what lies behind this. You should do it alone and together with your partner.

As we have mentioned before, one of the prerequisites for the acknowledging intimacy is your own interest in understanding why you feel and think the way you do about yourself and that you are able to understand your child's experiences and thoughts about what you say and do.

It is not possible to follow the process of the Acknowledging Dialogue with children, but we can use the principles and the philosophy of the dialogue, in the best sense of the word, to develop an "acknowledging" attitude towards our children. What follows is a description of ways in which you can develop an acknowledging attitude to conversation with children.

STOP AND THINK BEFORE YOU CRITICIZE AND SCOLD

When you are about to criticize and correct your child, wait a minute and notice on which cogwheel you are at that moment.

1. If you are on the large cogwheel, you may well tell your child in a considered and calm way what it is you want him or her to do. You may also be able to consider whether your child is ready to receive your message right now, or what you might do to get your child's attention.

2. If, on the other hand, you are about to jump on to the small cogwheel, you may be about to lose control. You tell your child what to do in no uncertain terms, or withdraw in anger and give up, depending on the survival strategies you have in your baggage. Relating to your child in this way will immediately trigger the child's survival strategies, and then the trouble begins. When feelings take over, then we parents need to learn how to make the all-important change of gears in order to restore the connection and create new understanding with our child.

Even though we know criticism is not the best way to meet our child, we all criticize sometimes. When this happens, it is useful to be clear about whether we are criticizing how our children are behaving or who they are. The main difference between criticizing your child for what he or she does, as opposed to what kind of human being he or she is, is usually in the depth of feeling attached to the criticism. We all know this from experience. When we are criticized for something we do – *It is a damned nuisance that you arrive an hour later than we agreed* – we can bear that, and most probably we will not have a problem taking it on board. But when we are criticized for who we are – *You can never be trusted and you never stick to your appointments* – we will hear the criticism quite differently. Regardless of the circumstances, time, place, and our state of mind, we will be hurt by this kind of criticism, as it comments on who we are as human beings.

The same phenomena occur with children who are in the process of developing their self-esteem. For this reason, we need to be extra careful of how we communicate criticism to our children.

Do we direct our criticism towards their behaviour, or is our criticism directed at them as human beings? There is a profound difference between saying: *I think it is annoying that you do not take your lunch box out of your schoolbag, when that is what we agreed,* and: *You make and break so many promises and what happens with the lunch box? Can't you be trusted? Not at all. It is just so disgusting that you leave it there in your backpack.*

When you are able to notice your part in a situation and take your share of responsibility for what is happening – the fact that YOU get annoyed – only then is there a hope that something different could happen to the lunch box in the future.

PRAISE IS A ROSE WITH THORNS

Often, we give praise when what our children really need from us is acknowledgement. Often, we do not think about whether we are praising or acknowledging our child. But there is an important difference. When we give praise, we usually want to honour something the child is doing, and we often start out with the sentence, *You are such a clever boy,* or *How wonderful it is to see that you . . .*

Your child may, for instance, have made a drawing, or received the top mark for an essay, and we give praise . . . *That is just marvellous . . .* However, we do not necessarily consider that every time we praise in this way, we may inadvertently be conveying to the child that what concerns us most is his or her performance. We also, by omission, convey what does not concern us and what we find insignificant – for instance, what the child experienced while doing the drawing or attending the exam, or what we thought or felt while looking at the drawing or exam mark.

Intentionally, we might send the message to our children that what matters most to us as parents is that they perform with excellence and that the result must be beautiful, great, right, etc. So, in this context, it may seem to them that it is less important that they feel good about themselves and their surroundings, that they feel calm and joyful, and that the things they do satisfy them.

CLEVER PETER

Ten-year-old Peter tells his father that he has thought a lot about the fact that time is a strange factor – present, past and future. Peter shares how he is thinking and his father answers Peter something like this: *It is clear that you have given the matter some serious thought. That makes me proud of you as a father.*

A couple of days later, Peter returns and tells his father that he has given a lot of thought to the question of how the earth was created. Again Peter offers a lengthy explanation. This time his father thinks that Peter's ideas are much less coherent and quite disconnected. So, when Peter has completed his explanation, he looks up at his father and asks: "Am I still clever now, daddy?" It dawns on Peter's father that, inadvertently, he has caused Peter's focus to shift from curiosity about the world he lives in to being clever. The father realizes that he is responsible for shifting Peter's focus from the contents of his thoughts to the question of performance – being clever.

When we give our children too much praise and focus on performance, then we forget simply to be present in the moment. This means that we parents miss opportunities to be in close connection with our children at any given moment. If, instead, we just acknowledge and describe what we are thinking and feeling when we are with our child, then we are automatically being in the present, in the here and now with the family. This means that we are then able to have more meaningful discussions of how the earth was created, or why an essay is awarded top mark.

Acknowledging conversations might sound like:

I become happy when I see that you . . .

I think you have some interesting thoughts. I am thinking I would like to . . .

How splendid that you got such a good mark! You must have really made an effort. I am pleased and proud.

In this way, we make it quite clear to our children and to ourselves whether or not we are connecting. *I see you, I notice something, and I tell you about it. I am also able to acknowledge you when we disagree.* In these ways, we communicate clearly to our children. This clarity is what children and young people need. The clarity also signals that we are able to convey which thoughts, feelings, and beliefs are our own, and which belong to our children. Sadly, many excellent opportunities for a good conversation founder when the parents hide behind a questioning *okay?* or behind lots of questions which do not allow a dialogue to begin.

SLOW DOWN!

It is a sign of the times that we are fast. Often, we are also far too quick when communicating with our children. We have neither the time nor the patience to wait for our children to finish telling us about the events of their day. But when we do, we give our children the space to relax, decrease the pace of their own stream of words, and savour events. It is important that we teach our children to be able to tolerate and, later, appreciate, silences in conversations and closeness. Lively, nurturing, and reciprocal dialogue always includes what we call turn taking. Here, we take turns being a storyteller and being a listener. Taking turns is not characterized, for instance, by statements such as: *Now I have listened to you, so it is your turn to listen to me talk about something completely different.* Turn taking means that we connect with each other's ideas. Our responses do not necessarily have to be detailed and they might, for instance, just consist of statements such as: *That sounds interesting. That makes me think of . . .*, or *Okay, you think that we should build a circular railway track. Good idea.*

When we wait for the child's response, we are creating a situation that is the equivalent of crossing the bridge to our child and following at his or her pace. Conversely, we sometimes respond too quickly and interrupt in order to tell our own story or offer our opinion. This can be seen as going back across the bridge to our own world.

TALK ABOUT WHAT YOU SEE YOUR CHILD IS DOING

Describe what you see your child is doing and comment on what he or she says – and continue to do this for the rest of your life! It is in this way that we see the unequivocal value of the mirroring process, which we can use in so many ways and situations with people.

You are laughing, you look happy . . .
I see this saddens you . . .
Look, there is Fido, he is coming towards us now . . .

Naturally your response needs to match the vocabulary of the age group. So, we do not tell our one-year-old child: *Look, here comes the neighbour's dog, a mix between a wirehaired fox terrier and a West Highland terrier.* Likewise, it does not make sense to say to your twelve-year-old son, *I see that you are brushing your teeth.*

When we comment on our children's actions from a very early age and talk to them about what they do, this can positively influence the child's development on many levels. When we offer our children words that describe what they do, see, hear, feel, and sense, we are giving them a great opportunity to get to know themselves. It is precisely this connection between language, action, emotions, and thoughts that provide children – and also adults – with the opportunity for the brain to develop in the best possible way and to get to know ourselves and our environment. When we voice our children's feelings, without confusing them with our own views or emotions by, for instance, seeming unappreciative or disapproving, then we are helping children to understand themselves and to dare to be themselves.

When we tell children that we can see and take note of what they feel, particularly if those feelings are strongly felt, then we convey to them that even if the feelings are violent and difficult to handle, it is all right to have them. Even more important, we do not disappear because of these feelings. Children receive from us the important message that it is all right to have a full range of feelings and that there are no right or wrong emotions.

AVOID TOO MANY QUESTIONS

Another reason to acknowledge what our children do and tell us is that when we do so, we do not need automatically to ask questions. Here we are talking about questions that our child may not be able, or want, to answer. For instance: *What have you done today? Are you drawing? What are you drawing? When did you come home? Who started the fight?*

Questions like these do not encourage dialogue. Children tend not to respond to questions by offering stories of what they did in kindergarten or at the party.

We may also need to notice how often we transform what is a comfortable and relaxed situation with our child, where we might be reading aloud from a book, to a situation full of demands because we suddenly start to ask questions. We might, for instance, fall into the trap of seeing if the child has got the page numbers in the book right. When we do this, we lose the original purpose of our time together: reading aloud. Our child may also lose his or her concentration and interest in being with us, change the subject, and then start fidgeting in his or her chair, talking about something altogether different. We don't understand why, and may begin to blame our child: *You should sit still, remember we are reading a book*, or *Now you will soon be four years old, so you will be big enough to sit still for a little longer.*

We have created a bad atmosphere with all our questions . . .

An additional point that should be mentioned is that commentary, rather than asking questions, is much more effective in relation to children's language development. The best way to teach children to talk is to talk to them about all kinds of things – objects, people, situations, animals, and emotions – instead of asking them if they know the words for this or that. So, instead of asking, for instance, *What are you eating?*, it would be much more appropriate to the child's language development to say: *I see that you are eating pasta as well as meat and broccoli.*

TALK ABOUT WHAT YOU ARE DOING

Remember to put words to what you are doing, thinking, feeling, and sensing. Of course, we do not mean everything, but all the things which you think would be interesting to the child. This will depend, among other things, on your child's age, your relationship with your child, as well as the actual activity you are sharing.

There are some general considerations we would like to draw to your attention. When we talk about what we are doing, we are inviting our children into our universe. So, in other words, we are making ourselves visible and transparent to our children.

You can, for instance, be very transparent to your young child when you say: *Now I will sit down here with you and then I will read you a book.*

We can be transparent with our children about our thoughts: *Right now I am thinking about my work and am not listening to everything you tell me.*

Finally, we can make ourselves transparent about our feelings and experiences: *I am glad that we are doing this together. When you hit me, I get angry.*

When we let ourselves be seen, we are making it possible for our children to connect with what we are doing, thus creating the basis for a relational connection. As parents, we should not just be reacting to our children. Rather, we should be authentic and bring our own thoughts and feelings into the relationship.

The more our children know about who we really are, the more secure will be our relationship with our children. Understanding what is going on for another person is a prerequisite for a relaxed relationship where we feel confident enough to be ourselves. When our children know how we feel and what we are thinking, they can be present with their entire personality. It is then that they do not have to worry about living up to our expectations about how we think things should be.

OFFER GUIDANCE WHENEVER POSSIBLE

Children need guidance from their parents. There are many life situations where there are some rules or structures which we want the child to learn to follow. Any normal day involves quite a number of situations where we have to comply with structure to a lesser or greater extent. Eating dinner together is such a situation, with certain rules and rituals that differ from family to family. Lots of families have in common that it matters how you eat together. In addition, there can be many situations during a day when the child is required to learn something new and needs guidance: brushing your teeth in the morning, leaving home on time, the importance of drinking plenty of water, etc.

As we have said, the keyword in these situations is offering guidance to our children. This means that we say clearly what we expect our children to do in any given situation. The younger the child, the more detailed the guidance needs to be. If our guidance is to be a real support to the child, it needs to be relevant to what is happening here and now. This means that we need to match the guidance we offer to fit the child's pace and developmental stage. Often, we adults are too quick in offering our guidance. We can be impatient, busy, or stressed, and, therefore, lose our grip on what otherwise could be calm and "well-timed" guidance. Instead, we might become annoyed, or get into a mood that can sometimes result in our using a hard tone of voice, or delivering a full-blown scolding.

Let's get on with it. It cannot be as difficult as all that. You must pull yourself together. Can't you understand that we are busy? How many times do I have to tell you that . . .

When we ensure that we have time and are calm when guiding our children through any number of demanding daily situations, then we will get better results. To start with, our children will feel successful in their diverse activities and have a feeling of mastering life challenges with expert support in a friendly and acknowledging atmosphere. What this means is that in every individual situation where he or she is successful, he or she is also having an experience of co-operation. It is through these experiences that we provide the basis for our child's belief about him or herself as a human being capable of combining demands and challenges with pleasure and co-operation. When this does not happen, our child will feel that certain of life's demands are associated with power struggles and a bad atmosphere in the form of criticism and scolding.

SUDDENLY MOTHER BECAME LIKE A DIFFERENT PERSON

Magnus, aged sixteen, is very frustrated because his friends are away on summer holidays in a warmer climate. He is bored. He also wants to go to the Mediterranean and thinks that it is a rotten deal that his family cannot afford to travel to the ends of the earth. As a result, he does not want to go anywhere, even if his family is going to a summerhouse on the island of Samsoe and then spending a week in London. The only thing he feels like doing is going on holiday with some friends, but they have all left him. During previous holidays, he has always followed through on ideas and arranged activities: for instance, taking friends to the summerhouse on the island of Samsoe or on a canoe trip. His mother Karen's first reaction is exasperation. She has had enough of the fact that Magnus is so cross and uninterested in making agreements with friends when that is what he says he wants. No matter what suggestions Karen comes up with, he does not want to go – whether to the Samsoe music festival, where there are plenty of other teenagers, or a holiday in a European capital, where Karen can borrow a flat.

Karen and Magnus discuss this issue on and off for several days, and Karen begins to feel quite powerless. She doesn't like the idea that a sixteen-year-old should be on his own for six weeks of summer vacation. However, she does not want to force him into anything either. Karen also feels sad that there should be this conflict, since this might be the last summer holiday they share for a while – in the future, Magnus probably will arrange holidays with his friends.

Karen also discusses this with her husband, who is not Magnus's biological father. He listens to her concerns and tries to understand why the conflict troubles her so much. Perhaps some old stories are involved? In fact, the scenario reminds Karen of episodes in her own youth when she was forced to participate in various family activities against her will. Her father would, for instance, completely ignore her attempts at protest. He would just say that the parents' decision could not be discussed. Karen recalls the feeling of being "railroaded" by her family, and that her father was apparently completely indifferent to her wishes and opinions.

Karen does not want Magnus to have the same experience. To prevent the conflict from escalating, Karen decides to take an alternative action. Her suggestions have obviously not led to any resolution. Karen decides to acknowledge Magnus's feelings and tells him that she understands that he has outgrown family holidays. Playing in the beautiful landscape on Samsoe and going for a swim in the evening are no longer attractive options. She wishes that she had some "holiday millions" and could fulfil his wildest vacation dreams.

Soon, Magnus changes the subject and begins to talk about how difficult it has been for him to make new friends at grammar school. He feels like an outsider. Moreover, he is not pleased with his looks. He has a lot of pimples and spends a fortune on remedies to clear up his skin. He also eats healthy food, but to no avail. Suddenly, a completely new subtext to the conflict emerges. Karen listens attentively until Magnus has finished talking.

Karen says that she understands perfectly well how frustrating it is to him that the pimples persist even though he eats healthy food, avoids sweets and junk food, and cares for his skin with expensive lotions. It is just not fair.

Magnus continues and says that he constantly worries about looking spotty, and that his friends probably notice. For the first time, Karen senses how much this bothers him. She says it must be distressing and frustrating for him to constantly have to think about his looks and other people's thoughts about his looks.

Karen asks if he would like to hear what she thinks about his story. He nods assent. Karen says that she thinks that there is much more to him than his looks. She voices her appreciation for his human qualities. His bright mind and sensitivity, among other things. This enables Magnus to empathize with other people and understand how they are thinking. This is an amazing ability to have, and Karen says that she is actually very proud of having a son like him. Finally, she is very appreciative that he opens up and shares his thoughts and feelings. Karen tells him that it is very brave of him to come out and tell her about his vulnerability in such a direct way.

Magnus ends the conversation with a smile and says that he is very pleased with what Karen told him. He feels better now, and is thinking about asking his old friend Rune to join them when they go to London. He thinks this is an excellent idea. Karen is very relieved that she is now in touch with Magnus again after a period of many escalation crises. She is extremely pleased that Magnus has, in fact, succeeded in finding a solution that is workable for him.

THE STORY FROM MAGNUS'S PERSPECTIVE

The summer holidays got off to a bad start. All my friends went on Mediterranean holidays and I just did not want to be in Denmark. I, too, wanted to go to the sun, because I could not handle another rainy summer – it drains me of energy. I usually have holiday activities lined up with my friends, but this year I had not got round to making any plans. In fact, I had a problem asking my new mates at grammar school if they were interested in planning some-thing together, as I was a little worried that they would say no. The last couple of years I have had so many pimples and skin problems, and that preoccupies me. All I can think of is how to get rid of the pimples. I buy expensive ecological skin lotions and ages ago I made up my mind to eat only healthy food and stay away from sugar. But nothing works.

Because of my skin problem, I have very low self-esteem at the moment. I feel as if other people are constantly staring at me and thinking that I look awful. My father says that he also looked like that at my age and that it is a genetic thing . . . I just think it is unfair. Lately, my mother has become quite a busybody. She has constantly been asking me questions about what I want to do in my holiday and if I feel like bringing a friend along. She has been so annoying. I would prefer to stay home alone, but I am not allowed to. However, yesterday she was suddenly OK. She stopped asking about all kinds of issues. We discussed the holidays again and I told her why it is no longer as easy as it was to have a good holiday. She listened to what I had to say, and said that she understood how I felt. She also said some positive things – for instance, that she thinks I am rather good at understanding how other people feel. I was very pleased about that and then I suddenly felt like asking Rune if he would like to come along to London. At that point, all the worries about how I look became less important.

GOOD RULES-OF-THUMB

1. When other friends, family, and colleagues confront
    me with frustrations about my parenthood or my child
    or if I am frustrated by other people's ways of
    parenting:

    -   I listen and mirror, until the other person has
        completed his or her story;

    -   I acknowledge the other person's experience;

    -   I say how the story affects me;

    -   I say to the other person what he or she could best
        do to help me with the process of talking about my
        child.

2. When I want to talk about my own frustration in
    relation to the ways in which other people do their
    parenting:

    -   I ask if I can talk about something that frustrates
        me, something which deals with the other person's
        way of parenting or with the child's behaviour;

    -   I make suggestions as to how we could talk about it;

    -   I talk about the frustration, and in particular about
        what the frustration does to me;

    -   I avoid criticizing the other person;

    -   I maintain an acknowledging and empathic attitude
        to the other person's response to my frustration.

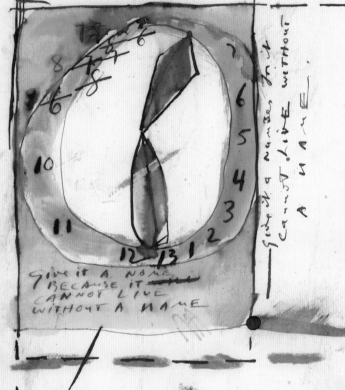

SECONDS TO THIRD QUALITY WORK

Give it a name because it cannot live without a name.

GIVE IT A NAME
BECAUSE IT
CANNOT LIVE
WITHOUT A NAME

Hanns Niessen

ACKNOWLEDGING RELATIONSHIPS
WITH GRANDPARENTS

When we become parents, it is often quite natural that the grandparents move closer to a family with young children. This can be a great support, but many have probably also experienced how this can have a disturbing effect and cause conflicts.

There can be an imbalance between welcoming support and closeness and suffocating offers of help. The impact of any such lack of balance will depend on how much insecurity we carry with us in our baggage.

Often, the grandparents show a remarkable degree of tolerance and greater understanding of their grandchildren than they were able to show towards their own children. It can seem contradictory and even painful to see how our parents are capable of giving to our children all the things we longed for when we were children.

There will also be all the remarks and the "good advice" from grandparents to us as parents, which reminds us of scenarios we experienced as children and which we would prefer not to repeat and with which we disagree . . . *you will regret going to her at the slightest cry . . . when you were children you were not allowed to dominate the conversation at the dinner table the way Agnete does* . . . For many reasons, there will be lots of opportunities for disagreements about how to raise children.

Throughout our lives, we go through phases of separation from our parents. First, the "terrible twos", then adolescence, and later, when we move away from the parental home, we choose careers, partners, and homes of our own. Becoming parents is yet another phase in the emancipation from our parents. Acknowledgement is needed from all sides.

As parents, it is a challenge for us to try to remain in an equal relationship with our own parents. We are up against strong forces. When we are new parents, there is every good reason to steer clear of unnecessary conflicts, irritations, or disagreements that can hurt our children and our relationship.

As with all other relationships, we start from the position that we all thrive and develop best in an acknowledging and intimate space. When we succeed in maintaining this kind of space between us as parents, the next step is to create a similar space of acknowledgement and mutual respect with our own parents – the grandparents. We need to recognize and acknowledge their stage in life as grandparents and remember to be clear about what our own needs and wishes are as parents.

IS THIS POSSIBLE ON A DAILY BASIS?

In many families, we try to create traditions around special occasions. In addition to birthdays and holidays, there might be a Sunday family dinner, a day once a week when the grand-children are routinely collected from their day-care centre to spend some time with the grandparents, or there might be the occasional weekend sleep-over with grandparents.

But who negotiates the events and relationships, and can we, as parents, ensure that there is an acknowledging emotional atmos-phere? In our view, attempting to be present to our children – and to our parents – offers the best opportunity to maintain awareness of differences and the importance of being either a listener or a storyteller in our conversations. This is imperative, even if it is easier said than done! However, when we manage to create an acknowledging space between ourselves as parents and grandparents, then our children are in their element, feeling free, confident, and adventurous.

When we are preoccupied with parenting, we sometimes can forget that if we want the grandparents to be significant others for our children, we also have to take the responsibility to include them in our family life.

Try to go back in time. Many of us have had a very special and significant relation with a grandparent. In order to pass this experience on to our own children, we need to take the initiative and create the necessary space to allow contact to flourish. This is just like the breast-feeding mother who needs to consciously share the responsibility with the father. So, it is also of crucial importance that the grandparents feel included at an early stage, and that they have the opportunity for regular reliable contact. If, from day one, we experience that our own parents or parents-in-law offer their help with a genuine interest and an unconditional love, that makes us feel quite confident about handing over the children to them. This means that the grandparents have the opportunity to develop their own very special bond with the children. The confidence emerges when they sustain the contact.

It can be a challenge to the parents to create a space where the independent contact between grandparents and grandchildren can be created. Parents also have the responsibility to protect their children from damaging criticism or negativism. As parents, we should try to ensure that grandparents feel they can be honest and speak openly about conflicts or problems with the grandchildren. If we parents are able to maintain a listening and acknowledging attitude with the grandparents, as well as with the children, then we are operating on the large cogwheel and can suggest different responses the grandparents can make the next time they run into conflict with the grandchildren.

GRANDMOTHER INTERFERES

Pia and Peter are on holiday with their two children, Rasmus, aged three, and Mette, aged eight, and Pia's parents. One evening during dinner, Rasmus crawls around under the table instead of eating his food. When this has been going on for some time, granny tells him that he should sit at the table when they eat. Rasmus sulks, and first he climbs up on to his mother's lap, and then down on to the floor under the table again. The conversation at the table continues, but the atmosphere is rather strained. It seems a little difficult to create the friendly and cheerful atmosphere everyone wants to enjoy.

Later in the evening, in order to get to grips with what happened at the dinner table, Pia and Peter go through an Acknowledging Dialogue in their attic room. Pia is frustrated by the way in which granny intervenes, but she is also frustrated by the fact that she is not taking a stand, as she would like to avoid a bad atmosphere at the table. Pia is aggravated by the way in which Rasmus constantly challenges her by wanting his own way and to set the agenda. At home, he does not do this to the same extent, because Pia manages to talk him out of it. Pia also gets annoyed when he whimpers, sulks, or cries and feels sorry for himself. Pia sees herself getting into the power struggle and saying: *Either you come to me to be comforted or else you go outside.*

In fact, Pia is not afraid either of Rasmus' anger or his tears. What she fears is her own annoyance and rejection of Rasmus, and for this reason she often feels she goes too far. Then Pia neither manages to say stop nor does she set other limits. Pia fears that she could get annoyed like her mother used to do. For this reason, Pia withdraws into herself and her frustrations mount.

The same pattern unfolds in Pia's relationship with Peter. When Peter complains about something, Pia gets annoyed and withdraws – not in order to reject him, but to avoid a bad atmosphere and the negative spiral. Pia's acknowledging intimacy with Rasmus and Peter is now interrupted. Pia realizes that Rasmus, too, has developed a pattern where he believes he can set the agenda. Clearly, he has not yet learnt to accept or live with a no. Until now, Pia has been able to coax Rasmus out of these power struggles.

In the Acknowledging Dialogue, Pia suggests that they support each other in setting some limits, which they work out together. Pia and Peter also decide that they will revisit the granny situation at the dinner table. They want her to know that they understand how important it is for her that everyone be seated at the table in order to share and eat food together. They also want granny to know that they have discussed this issue and are aware that Rasmus is at a developmental stage where they know they need to set more limits. They are going to be clear with Rasmus that they want him to stay seated in his chair during mealtime, and they want him to let them know when he has finished eating. Either Pia or Peter will then take Rasmus outside to play without restraint, and the meal can continue peacefully. Granny is enthusiastic about this proposal: she is relieved, and it helps her to know that Pia and Peter have a plan they intend to follow. Granny would like to support them and play her part in the plan.

It is so important that we parents understand that the entire emotional atmosphere in the room is crucial for our children, not just in the nuclear family, but with any of the significant people in our lives. It is vital to children that they feel that the adults voice different opinions and even disagree, and still stay well connected to one another. If there are unvoiced disagreements concerning the children, then the children feel divided loyalties and believe that they have to take sides. So, what is an adult difference of opinion can then become a problem to the child.

When there is tension in relationships between us and our parents, we need to revisit our own stories in an Acknowledging Dialogue with our partner. Not taking the time to dialogue means frustration followed by survival strategies, creating more confusion and distance in our relationships with our partners and our children. By keeping in mind the acknowledging intimacy and the Acknowledging Dialogue, we can, as parents, restore intimacy and confidence in our relationship.

SKETCH (ROUGH) FOR C A R T O O N

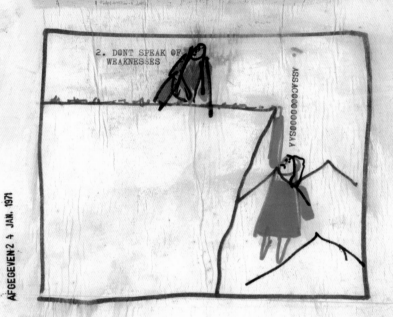

2. DONT SPEAK OF
WEAKNESSES

AFGEGEVEN 2 4 JAN. 1971

C A R T OO N
R O U G H

THE NEW AMSTERDAM SCHOOL
OF IKON PAINTING
(SHIPS) T/O AMSTEL 49 BIJ WATERLOOPLEIN
AMSTERDAM - HOLLAND

8 2

DER TIENDE BOEK
* PLEASE DO *
NOT

THE LOGBOOK
OF THE SHIP
"HENRY DAVID THOREAU"

the "Diamond–CRAFT" cooking pot
(made in Los Angeles)

YELLOW

wood

wood

EAT POT

Hot

red

UP AND DOWN

FROM THE

BOTTOM

thick
aluminium
alloy

Sunday 30 Aug. 1970

which came to Walter in 1950 was
lost in 20 ft. water in Jamaica & Re-
covered By Rolf (woof) in Summer 1953 —
comes to Be the Pot of the EAT Box 1970
& thrown into the Amstel River by the
Jesus Hole & returned this morning

78

NEDERLAND
1 CENT

ACHTSTE BOEK
PLEASE ADMIT
* ONE *
ELEPHANT

POSTSCRIPT

We are now reaching our journey's end and are about to reach the last page. Parenthood, however, is an on-going process. We will be the parents of our children for the rest of our lives, and perhaps we will also be fortunate enough to become grandparents.

All parents hope that their adult children will be able to tell the story of a happy childhood with them. We want our children to tell a story that confirms that we have been good enough parents. However, deep down, we know full well that the story is never that black and white. We hope that, through reading this book, you will dare to risk listening to your children's stories about what it was and is like living with you. The book encourages you as the reader to "cross the bridge" and hear what it was really like to be a child in the family which you and your partner created. Risking being vulnerable to hearing how the small events of daily life were experienced and what made an impression can enrich your lives. When your children feel safe enough to tell you how they think situations could have been improved, you are all living in acknowledging intimacy. Accepting the challenge to feel the pain of not having succeeded in the past as well as we might today, with the knowledge and understanding we have now, can only strengthen our relationships and help us live more authentic lives.

Given our knowledge about how important and enriching it is to dare to face reality from your child's perspective, we can afford to be optimistic about our parenting. Sofie and her son Kasper, aged twenty-one, confirm this. In an Acknowledging Dialogue, Kasper told the following story about how difficult it was for him to grow up with his parent's regular disagreements about how to bring him up. In the dialogue, he tells his mother Sofie the following:

"I remember that you occasionally bought me some toys – for instance, a special box of Lego. Of course, I was pleased, but I also remember that it came at a price. When father came home from work and asked you what you had bought for me and what it had cost, then the trouble began. You started quarrelling in front of me and I remember that the word 'spoilt' was used. I remember and still feel that I believed that it was my fault that my parents were fighting again. With the knowledge I have today, I can see what a strain it was to feel that I was the source of my parents' fights. I felt a huge weight of responsibility on my shoulders.

"Today, I realize that it would have been a help if you, as my parents, had taken responsibility for your disagreements and kept me out of them. Father could, for instance, have said:

Kasper, go and play with your new box of Lego. I understand that you are pleased with it. Your mother and I disagree about the size of the gifts we should buy. Mother and I will sort that out between the two of us – it's not your problem."

Naturally, it is difficult to hear such a story from your adult child, but it can also be a release and enrich our lives. The point is not that we as adults should feel criticized and need to protect ourselves from blame, but that we should allow ourselves to reflect on our children's experiences and longings. From another point of view, being interested in hearing from your child what it was like having you as a parent enables our children to create a more coherent story about their childhood. Whether our children's memories are of positive or painful experiences, the most important thing is that they are able and daring enough to share them with you. We can be sure that when our adult children are able to share and understand their story and the connections between various events, they will have the opportunity to live their lives differently. In the dialogue Kasper was having with his mother, he was asked what story he would like one day to hear from his child. He said, among other things, that he would like to hear:

"One of the things that has made me extremely happy is that my parents have always shown how much they love each other."

In fact, openness and acknowledging intimacy can make it easier to accept that we cannot be perfect parents or grandparents, and nor should we want to be. Acknowledging intimacy can help us develop our authenticity and ability to be fully present in relationships from generation to generation . . .

BONNIE'S BRILLEN

writing the Lesson of the EYEGLASSES

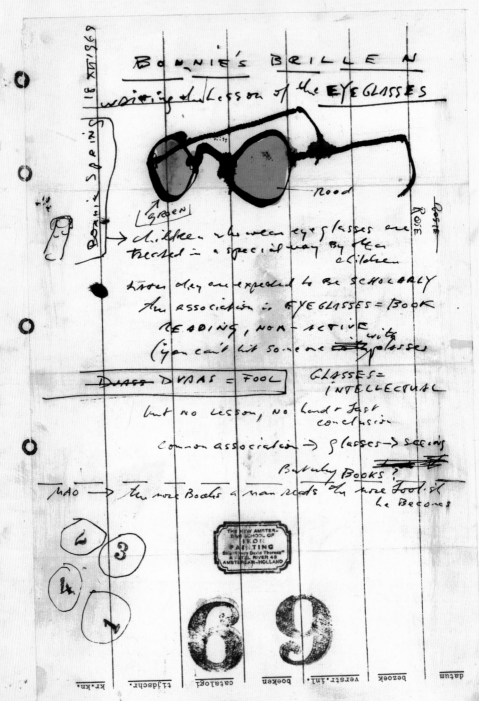

Bonnie Springs

16 XII 1969

→ GREEN   Rood   Rose Rosé

→ children who wear eyeglasses are treated in a special way by other children

Know they are expected to be SCHOLARLY
An association is EYEGLASSES = BOOK
READING, NON - ACTIVE
(you can't hit someone with eyeglasses

~~Dumas~~ DUMAS = FOOL   GLASSES = INTELLECTUAL

but no lesson, no hard + fast conclusion

Common association → Glasses → seeing

Berkeley BOOKS?

MAO → the more Books a man reads the more Foolish he becomes

① ② ③ ④ ⑦

THE NEW AMSTER-
DAM SCHOOL OF
IKOK
PAINTING
Ship "Henry David Thoreau"
A Joyel RIVER 49
AMSTERDAM-HOLLAND

69

REFLECTIONS

For parents:

1. Consider what kind of story about childhood and youth you would like your child to tell you one day. Share your thoughts with your partner.

2. Consider what it would mean to you to hear from your child stories that are painful to hear. Share your thoughts with your partner.

3. Consider how you can support each other and your child in remaining open to painful narratives and seeing them as experiences and stories rather than criticism. Share your thoughts with your partner.

4. Share your thoughts with your partner about the ways in which you would like your own parents and parents-in-law to give their continued support to you as parents – and how you might broach this with them.

For grandparents:

1. You are worried and perhaps annoyed by an experience you have had with your adult child's family/child/partner. Share that with your partner and imagine how you might invite your child to cross the bridge for an Acknowledging Dialogue about your concerns.

2. You feel sad about something in your own life. Share this with your partner and discuss whether you should share it with your adult child, and if so, how.

BIBLIOGRAPHY

THE VIBRANT FAMILY
Dencik, L., Jørgensen, P. S., & Sommer, D. (2008). *Familie og Børn i en opbrudstid*. Copenhagen: Hans Reitzels Forlag (Danish edition).

Gottman, J., & Silver, N. (2003). *The Seven Principles for Making Marriage Work*. London: Orion House.

Seidenfaden, K., & Draiby, P. (2011). *The Vibrant Relationship*. London: Karnac.

WHEN LOVERS BECOME PARENTS
Schibbye, A.-L. L. (2005). *Relationer – et dialektisk perspektiv*. Copenhagen: Akademisk Forlag (Danish edition).

Sommer, D., Pramling Samuelsson, I., & Hundeide, K. (2010). *Child Perspectives and Children's Perspectives in Theory and Practice*. Germany: SpringerVerlag.

ATTACHMENT AND EXPLORATION IN FOCUS
Bowlby, J. (1988). *A Secure Base*. New York: Basic Books.

Gerhard, S. (2004). *Why Love Matters*. London: Brunner Routledge.

Holmes, J. (2001). *The Search for the Secure Base – Attachment Theory and Psychotherapy*. London: Routledge.

Johnson, S. M. (Ed.), & Whiffen, V. E. (2003). *Attachment Processes in Couple and Family Therapy*. New York: Guilford Press.

Rholes, S. W., & Simpson, J. A. (2004). *Adult Attachment*. New York: Guilford Press.

Siegel, D. J., & Hartzell, M. (2003). *Parenting From the Inside Out*. New York: Penguin Group.

Stern, D. J. (1985). *The Interpersonal World of the Infant*. New York: Basic Books.

THE BRAIN – OUR INVISIBLE GREENHOUSE
Cozolino, L. (2006). *The Neuroscience of Human Relationships*. New York: Norton.

Damasio, A. (2000). *The Feelings of What Happens – Body, Emotion, and the Making of Consciousness*. New York: Vintage Books.

Hart, S. (2010). *The Impact of Attachment (Norton Series on Interpersonal Neurobiology)*. New York: Norton, Kindle Edition.

Kringelbach, M. L. (2004). *Hjernerum – Den følelsesfulde hjerne*. Copenhagen: Peoples Press (Danish edition).

LeDoux, J. (1998). *The Emotional Brain*. New York: Phoenix.

LeDoux, J. (2002). *Synaptic Self – How Our Brains Become Who We Are*. New York: Penguin.

Mayes, L., Fonagy, P., & Target, M. (2007). *Developmental Science and Psychoanalysis*. London: Karnac.

Reddy, V. (2008). *How Infants Know Minds*. New York: Harvard University Press.

Siegel, D. J. (1999). *The Developing Mind*. New York: Guilford Press.

THE TRANSFORMATIVE POWER OF STORYTELLING

Anderson, H. (1997). *Conversation, Language and Possibilities*. New York: Basic Books.

Gergen, K. (1994). *Realities and Relationships*. New York: Harvard University Press.

Gergen, K. (1999). *An Invitation to Social Construction*. London: Sage.

Morgan, A. (2000). *What is Narrative Therapy*. Melbourne: Gecko.

Morgan, A., & White, M. (2006). *Narrative Therapy With Children and Their Families*. Adelaide: Dulwich Centre Publ.

White, M. (2000). *Reflections on Narrative Practice*. Adelaide: Dulwich Centre Publ.

ACKNOWLEDGING INTIMACY IN OUR DAILY LIVES

Allen, J. G., & Fonagy, P. (Eds.) (2007). *Handbook of Mentalization-based Treatment*. Chichester: Wiley & Sons Ltd.

Buber, M. (1923). *Ich und du*. Martin Buber Estate (German edition).

Cooperider, C. F., Sorensen, P. F., Yeager, T. F., & Whitney, D. (Eds.) (2001). *Appreciative Inquiry: An Emerging Direction for Organisation Development*. New York: Stipes.

Fonagy, P., Gergely,G., & Target, M. (2007). *Affect Regulation, Mentalization and the Development of the Self*. London: Other Press.

Hayes, S. C., & Smith, S. (2008). *Get Out of Your Mind and Into Your Life: The New Acceptance and Commitment Therapy*. New York: New Harbinger Publ. Inc.

McNamee, S., & Gergen, K. J. (1999). *Relational Responsibility*. London: Sage.

Seligman, M. E. P. (2002). *Authentic Happiness*. New York: Free Press.

Stavros, J. M., & Torres, C. B. (2005). *Dynamic Relationships: Unleashing the Power of Appreciative Inquiry in Daily Living*. Ohio: Taos Institute.

Stern, D. J. (1985). *The Interpersonal World of the Infant*. New York: Basic Books.

THE ACKNOWLEDGING DIALOGUE

Hendrix, H., & Lakelly Hunt, H. (1997). *Giving the Love That Heals – A Guide for Parents*. New York: Pocket Books.

Holmes, J., & Bateman, A. (2001). *Integration in Psychotherapy. Models and Methods*. Oxford: Oxford University Press.

Honneth, A. (1995). *The Struggle for Recognition: The Moral Grammar of Social Conflicts*. Cambridge, MA: MIT Press.

Johnson, S. M. (2004). *Creating Connection – The Practice of Emotionally Focused Couple Therapy*. New York: Brunner-Routledge.

Rogers, C. (1967). *On Becomming a Person – a Therapist's View of Psychotherapy*. London: Constable & Company.

THE ACKNOWLEDGING DIALOGUE WITH CHILDREN

Øvreeide, H., & Hafstad, R. (1996). *The Marte Meo Method and Developmental Supportive Dialogues*. Eindhoven: Aarts Productions.
Sørensen, J. B. (2008). *Støt Mestring – Bryd Mønstre*. Copenhagen: Dafolo forlag (Danish edition).
Verheugt-Pleiter, A. J. E., Zevalkink, J., & Schmeets, M. G. J. (2008). *Mentalizing in Child Therapy*. London: Karnac.

SUBJECT INDEX